A Belle in the Prison of Socrates

A Belle in the Prison of Socrates

By

Ahmed Etman

Cambridge Scholars Publishing

A Belle in the Prison of Socrates, by Ahmed Etman

This book first published 2008 by

Cambridge Scholars Publishing

15 Angerton Gardens, Newcastle, NE5 2JA, UK

British Library Cataloguing in Publication Data
A catalogue record for this book is available from the British Library

ISBN (10): 1-84718-527-4, ISBN (13): 9781847185273

He put a white robe on his shoulder
And said as he overcame his tears:
"Please spare
The explanation and justification
For I hadn't known
That the evil Polyphemus
Is that cruel
In hurting and torturing
Of fathers and sons."
He put his white robe on his shoulder
And was bidden farewell by his dear sons
Without tears.

—A.E.

TABLE OF CONTENTS

Preface
Prof. Lorna Hardwick ix

Preface
Prof. Freddy Decreus xi

Introduction by the translator xv
Prof. Fawzia El-Sadr

Foreword xix

A Belle in the Prison of Socrates

Personae 3

Act One 5

Scene I: Socrates' Shoes are not for Sale 5
Scene II: The Price of Freedom 17
Scene III: Towards a Clean Environment 33
Scene IV: The worst calamity makes one laugh. .... .41

Act Two 53
Scene I: Waiting for the Defeat 53
Scene II: Victory of the Defeated 65
Scene III: The Real Beginning 82

PREFACE

LORNA HARDWICK, PROFESSOR OF CLASSICS THE OPEN UNIVERSITY

This is a drama that plays with the metaphorical stage of current debates as well as with its readers' and audiences' interests in the ancient world. Ahmed Etman is a distinguished classical scholar who is also a major voice in comparative literature and in translation, having supervised the new translation of Homer's *Iliad* into Arabic, published in 2004. As though this were not enough, he is also a creative writer whose plays take leading figures from antiquity and dramatize their relationships with their historical contexts and with the modern imagination in ways that shed light on both.

This play takes the Athenian thinker Socrates, the 'gad-fly of Athens', and follows his conversations at home, in the Agora, on the city walls of the defeated *polis* and in his eventual trial, imprisonment and execution at the behest of the restored democracy. The dramatic structure and idiom of the play draws on and reworks major classical sources on Socrates' life and thought. Etman contextualizes these in the themes of the war between the Athenians and the Spartans and the resulting disruptions of Hellenic social identity and unity amid the shifting alliances with Persia.

The scenes and the dialogue hold in tension the domestic, the civic and the international. Readers of Thucydides and Xenophon, Aristophanes, Andocides and Plato will find much to intrigue and amuse them. Genres are fluid and the witty interweaving of the ancient sources with allusions to contemporary issues such as the environment, drugs and the generation-gap allows historical narrative from the 'messengers' to merge with Socratic dialogue and dream sequences and so align ancient and modern. Noteworthy variations on the central theme play with temporalities to introduce Plato's journey to Egypt as a cultural encounter between Greek philosophy and Egyptian wisdom while Socrates is enabled to probe the relationship between law and popular demonstrations in the operations of Democratia.

Fawzia El- Sadr's translation of the play into English is timely in several respects. The increase in translations from Arabic into English is making available to anglophones a rich strand of literary culture. In the case of translations of work inspired by ancient Greek texts there is an increase in the potential for dialogues which cross cultural and linguistic boundaries yet are also grounded in ancient sources that are important in both cultures (see for example the four plays in *The Arab Oedipus*, edited by Marvin Carlson, New York, 2005). Furthermore, Etman's play marks an important addition to the corpus of dramatisations of Greek philosophy and historiography, a companion to John Barton's *The War That Still Goes On : Adapted from Thucydides' History of the Peloponnesian Wars and Plato's Dialogue with Alcibiades*, London, 2006 (which was also staged in a rehearsed reading in London in February 2006). The ancient texts and contexts are richly resonant for the contemporary world. Etman's dramatization teases readers and audiences to develop their own responses to both.

PREFACE

FREDDY DECREUS, PROFESSOR OF CLASSICS, UNIVERSITY OF GHENT BELGIUM

'Democratia herself in my prison', Socrates exclaims, wondering who that phantom may be that haunts him in the sudden absence of his guards! 'Socrates…you are a god Socrates', she replies.

Two these sentences, belonging to the last moments of Socrates in prison, reveal a lot. On the one hand, there is this man, a philosopher, dressed in rags, bare-footed, a louse on his bald-head, meditating in his last moments, not afraid to die. On the other hand, there is this woman called Democratia, symbol and allegory, representative of a culture based upon power, manipulation and deceit. She is trapped in a dilemma, since a revolt in Athens calls, in the days of the coming elections, for the release of Socrates, who recently has been convicted by a jury manipulated by Democratia herself. As a character belonging to the political arena, she represents just one of the many cheap and superficial humans, who do not understand at all what Socrates is dealing with.

A cross-reference to the *Magic Flute* of Mozart may help to situate this new play by Ahmed Etman as a drama recalling two totally different worlds where two kinds of heroes live: Tamino and Papageno. In terms of this play, the world of the spiritual and intellectual hero is only inhabited by Socrates, the other one by a number of secondary characters who are mainly interested in the lower pleasures of life: money, power, greed, manipulation,…. However, no matter how low and unsophisticated they have grown, they will fascinate the reader, since the animated dialogues between all kinds of characters, young and old, wise and less wise, will fascinate the reader and listener. Ahmed Etman who has studied a long time in Athens has a definite eye and ear for the way people in the street do their daily talk and gossip. The way the common people think and behave is rendered in a masterly way, old and new come together, Athens and Cairo fuse, the back streets of every big city offer a never ending spectacle that every dramatist wants to immortalize. In this new play, not only Democratia belongs to the second category: there is also Socrates' wife, called here Xanthula, reviving the old clichés of a nagging old bitch, you have former students who want to please the rulers, the guards in the prison, the maid Hedone,…

However, the many scenes that recall Plautinian boldness and vivacity and represent the outer appetising packing, cannot make forget the underlying seriousness. The professor of Classics and Comparative Literature that Ahmed Etman is, is so well read in the contemporary history of the Greek fifth century that one easily forget that most of the narrative details are based upon Greek texts. The Socrates that he resuscitates today is a brilliant compeer of the older version! This Socrates *redivivus* is rendered present in such a detailed way that the author really got in his skin, making forget the years of study it takes to perform such a deeply felt impersonation. Not a burden at all, these historical details provide in the first place good theatre, vivid discussions and quick-witted remarks that make the audience laugh!

From a political and sociological point of view, the times are ready for a drama like this, both in the old days and now. One may not forget that the era in which Socrates lived constituted a real hinge in the formation of Western intellectual and philosophic history. The matters are serious enough to be reconsidered. Socrates, above all, is the man who introduced theoretical discussions and who favoured knowing for the sake of knowing. His ambition was *theoria*, as later Aristotle would say, a form of pure and speculative knowledge, beyond human practical needs and interests. This ambition would lead him to disavow the survival of his own mortal body, and turned him into one of the first representatives of Humanism: what happened to be known later as 'theoretical man' started to question radically and unceasingly the conditions of knowing itself. No divinisation or humanisation of the forces of nature any more, no anthropomorphism to excuse the actions of pagan gods and goddesses. As a gad-fly, Socrates ran after his contemporaries, asking questions all the time, only satisfied when he succeeded in proving their lack of knowledge. Not an easy character after all, and the Athenians were not pleased at all to be confronted with 'philosophers': Anaxagoras (432) had to run, Protagoras (415) was accused under the same law indicting blasphemy and atheism. Socrates (399) was condemned, Plato pulled back for some time to Megara and travelled more than once to Syracuse, and even in 323 Aristoteles was accused. Apparently, those in power could hardly stand philosophers, but one cannot forget that out of this interaction a part of Western identity arose, precisely this part that invites people all over the world to step beyond personal profits and question the trans-personal, the universal.

A Belle in the Prison of Socrates is a play that brings back all these challenges, the first ones in the history of the West to question so deeply both our personal and collective identity. Although obviously written as a humorous tale about an extraordinary character called Socrates, a man not able to take care for his own socks and maintenance, this play also has deeper political tones that often enough expose a solid political criticism of superficial democracies. Definitely, a play with many faces, destined to intrigue different audiences!

INTRODUCTION

PROF. FAWZIA EL-SADR
AIN SHAMS UNIVERSITY, EGYPT

Are they really Socrates and his belle? And who is this "belle" is she a notion, or is she democracy aborted, or what? The title initiates the curiosity of the reader, for it sets him to question the concerns that the play presents. He is also skeptic about Socrates' belle, or probably even Socrates himself, who worries the Egyptian playwright at a difficult period when not only Egypt, and probably the Arab world and the whole world is going through, where the map is changing. And on reading the play, the reader realizes the confirmatory of his anticipations. True, the story of the play revolves around Socrates, as the plot springs forward, crystallizing this story in the form of events, within a framework that organizes them so as to allow space for the personae to conflict in such a manner, as to lead to a true expression of what the play proposes, or what is known as the "theme", in a way that reaches the reader, or the spectator, through deduction, rather than outspoken statements or bare ideas. Such a manner allows the "subject" or the message to emerge in a way, nearer to the sore finger, as is the case with many of the Egyptian plays, where you can easily locate the sentences conveying the theme, and which usually are overstated and which point openly at what the writer wishes to convey to the reader or spectator. Ahmed Etman did not overlook the style of the Greek philosopher Socrates that is characterized by dialoguing. His distinctive style of making dialogues depends on a method of deduction through insinuation, whereby he reaches the truth by cornering his interlocutor into reaching precisely what Socrates wants him to say, leading him on to admitting that very truth, spontaneously, naturally.

The play actually expresses the subject in the theatrical language and I do not refer here to the dialogue only, but I mean, the other theatrical techniques, such as story, plot, the events, time and place. However, it transcends Socrates and his society, environment and times, to touch on our contemporary society, through its characters, environment and times, in a manner that the reader or spectator cannot escape, for they focus on the manner that the human mind operates with the association of meanings. For the similarities between the ancient society of Socrates and the contemporary society, which the play emphasizes- in a successful selection- carries the play further to the level of the locale of our present times. The meeting or intercepting point between Athens and the present times carries the spectators, engaged in the events taking place in Athens to the current reality like a transit traveler then takes him back to Athens. And so on all throughout the play. True that the reader will watch Socrates and Xanthula and Democratia and Lysias and Chaerephon, as he will be convinced with them and their actions, However out of this foreign production, alternative contemporary replacement will unavoidably be stamped on his mind.

The play combines realism and fantasy. For the playwright escorts the reader on a journey between the present with its pains and the past where Socrates suffers from these around him whether it be his wife, or society itself, which makes the play a combination of the classical theatre and the modern experimental theatre, oscillating between past and present scenes in locale and personae: for human nature is pretty much the same in all ages. So that the reader finds himself on a journey, or an open invitation between, the contemporary society with its ailments, and the reality of the past and its ailments, A closer look into the text of the play confirms this double idea in its course, and which makes this "foreign" or Greek play, distant in its time and place, a local or contemporary play, closer to us in time and place. Let us look at some parts of this dialogue to emphasize this point.

> "Aristophanes: Today we enter into the depth of cultural hypocrisy and I will show you that men of letters and the intellectuals are inventing new terms, compatible with all ages, and coining titles by which they name every new ruler. This is 'an inspired leader' and another is 'a war and peace hero'. A third maker of 'historical geographical decisions'."

Socrates also accuses Democratia:

> "Whereas you and your relatives use the state's money and monopolize some privileges like trading in arms and lands and agricultural crops, and industrial goods local and imported and invest your money at the expense of the people's that you even sometimes import rotten food. "

He tells her "you claim to establish democracy and support its pillars, while you are obstinate in your opinion and forge the elections. You are like the malignant malady that destroys the body before a person can even feel it."

However, although the play apparently involves the ailments in classical Greece, it rises to universality, as it touches with subtlety human nature at all times, whether it be ancient Greece or the contemporary scene. What gives credit to *A Belle In The Prison Of Socrate*s, is that it shoots instantaneously in two harmonious levels like a double barrel rifle, carefully reaching its target.

FOREWORD

AHMED ETMAN

After my two plays "***Cleopatra Worships Peace***" and "***The Blind Guest Restores his Sight***" were published, I took to writing this play at hand in the mid eighties of the past century. In 1987, I reread the play, with view of making some alterations, these alterations developed into a new play, without making any essential changes in the play at hand. And so I had two plays with which I am not fully satisfied with. Finding myself in great perplexity I left them in closed drawers.

And in the summer of 2001 the matter recurred to me, so I took to reading this play once more, while bearing in mind an important female Athenian character—of this character I will not reveal now—and whom I had intended to add to the text, with view to intensifying its charm and excitement.

After a careful reading and a tiring revising, I found no place for this charming female character in the play. I felt that this play had fully matured, and standing as it is, does not tolerate the addition, that even the chosen title in the eighties survived of the number of titles that had subsequently occurred and recurred to me, so that after the necessary alterations this play "***A Belle in the prison of Socrates***" came to life to finally relieve its writer from prolonged labor pains.

To God we turn for success

A BELLE IN THE PRISON OF SOCRATES

Personae

Xanthula: The nickname of Xanthlippe rather plump, tall, pretty wife of Socrates.

Socrates: The famous philosopher, in his late sixties or early seventies.

Chaerephon: A friend of Socrates, almost his age.

Democratia: She represents the city of Athens and its political system; she is a middle-aged woman of moderate beauty and intelligence.

Maker of gods' statues: He is stout and clever in his craft, owns a shop in the public market. He wears a wreath over his head and rings in his fingers.

Ion: An epic Reciter, who sings heritage and forges it to the benefit of the ruler.

Aristophanes: The well-known comic poet in his forties; he collaborates in the play within the play.

The Peasant
Right
Wrong
} Characters in the play within the play.

Plato: Socrates' student during the early twenties.

Andocides: Solicitor and orator.

Lysias: Orator

Chief of guards: Tall, broad-shouldered, with a big mustache, tough and sullen.

Silent characters and various voices of Socrates' students, and public of men and women.

ACT ONE

Scene I

Socrates' Shoes are not for Sale

(Socrates' house. In the depth of the stage there are two walls: one on the right, with a door and a window overlooking the street, the other on the left, with a window leading to the inside. In the midst of the theatre is a primitive bed, on its side wooden stools. Socrates sits on a piece of stone beside the window of the right wall, in a state of contemplation. His wife Xanthula is sitting on the edge of the bed beside him, with a mirror in her hand, dressed in rich clothes and golden sandals, in contrast to Socrates, who is in tattered clothes and bare-footed).

Xanthula: The maid Hedone is out with the children for a walk, I asked her to do that. It's a chance for us to sit together…huh.

Socrates: ……

Xanthula: **(Sweetly)** Darling Socrates… Socrataki.

Socrates: ……

Xanthula: **(Raising her voice a bit)**Socrates… Socrataki.

Socrates: ……

Xanthula: **(Fretting, tapping the floor with her feet)** Socrates… Socrates.

Socrates: **(Facing her silently)**…..

Xanthula: **(Starring in the mirror as she cuddled her hair)** Didn't you hear me, sweetie… I said… we are alone, we can talk and…

Socrates: **(Interrupting)** Do you really want a dialogue… splendid! **(Getting up and approaching her)**

Xanthula: **(Cheerful)** Yes, I would like to have a dialogue alone with you…sometimes I even find my children a barrier between us… But today we are alone…so let's… **(Approaching him, trying to touch him or hug him, he withdraws)**

Socrates: If you want a fruitful dialogue, there must be an esthetic distance between us.

Xanthula: A distance! An esthetic distance between a married couple? O, catastrophe!

Socrates: Yes… so that none of us would affect the other…

Xanthula: And what fruitful dialogue could take place between a man and a woman with a distance between them? (**She approaches him as he ducks away**) All distances should disappear between husband and wife… they merge…an explosion takes place... a melting.

Socrates: Then this is not a dialogue.

Xanthula: But this is the most beautiful dialogue …come on. (**She is after him, he ducks away**)

Socrates: Anyway we should start a dialogue, whether it is a nearness you seek, or more differences and aloofness, as usual.

Xanthula: (**Sits on the bed, as Socrates stands in a distance**) Alright dear, it is time for you to prepare for the festivities.

Socrates: What festivities?

Xanthula: (**Surprised and astonished**) The great festivities of Dionysus. (**Adding**) They say that the competitions in theatre this year will be the strongest… for poets of tragedies, Sophocles and Euripides are taking part. (**Adding**) Anyway, I don't like tragedy… my eyes hurt out of crying when I watch them… I want to laugh, I like comedy… I am a pleasure-seeker. (**She gets up, approaches Socrates**) This year a young poet called Aristophanes will join the competition. They say that he wrote a wonderful play of funny situations… (**She places her hand on Socrates' shoulder sweetly, saying**) Everybody is getting ready for these festivities Socrates, and we have done nothing yet… (**Looking in Socrates' face to find that he is still absent-minded, she shakes him several times**) Did you listen to what I was saying… huh…

Socrates: (**Confused**) You were talking about… about…

Xanthula: (**Sarcastically**) About the sun, the moon, the clouds, the space… darling…huh

Socrates: I mean were you really talking about these matters? Then this is an interesting conversation! So, how do you see this superb universe and its enchanting system?

Xanthula: **(Impatiently)** My bitterness! No…I won't talk to you again. **(She walks away)**

Socrates: I told you over and over again that the conversation about these cosmological issues needs a long time and a lot of patience, so it would be more appropriate to deal with it out-doors in the fresh air… **(Getting up)**…come on… come on… let's go out to the mountain… climb to its peak …get closer to the clouds and discuss the system of the universe and its captivating beauty… Come on, I'm fed up with these closed places… they suffocate my breath and my thoughts… I feel as if I were in a prison…

Xanthula: Prison!! You say your life with me is a prison!! O catastrophe! Say you hate me too… you can't stand talking with me …and you need to get out to dialogue with your young wanderers students in the alleys… where you lecture them …I know you well… These lectures satisfy your vanity, because they make you appear as a dignified professor …but here with me you don't want to hear one word…you are unfair, just my bad luck. **(She is crying)**

Socrates: Anyway I'm going out.

Xanthula: **(Pulling herself together)** Over my dead body...you will never go out of here before you listen to me… **(Hedone, the maid enters carrying an infant and two boys...sons of Socrates)** or else I'll leave the house, the children…I'll go to my folks' place.

Socrates: **(Giving in)** My dear…no…don't do it…and don't be angry with me…here I'm listening to you, say what you want.

Xanthula: Wasn't I talking to you about the Dionysus festivities, they will be taking place soon and you aren't even prepared for them.

Socrates: Are they that soon?

Xanthula: They start in three days.

Socrates: And what am I to do?

Xanthula: Nothing…only remember that people receive these feasts and festivities in new clothes, change their old shoes with new ones and I'll buy you all that.

Socrates: But I didn't ask for anything.

Xanthula: **(In repressed boredom)** So will you be going to the festivities looking like that? In ragged clothes…bare-footed… aren't you ashamed of yourself? You brought me shame throughout Athens! Man, the whole down-town is but shoe-shops everywhere, and people say we can't afford to buy a pair.

Socrates: **(Sarcastic)** That is true, even book-stores have turned into shoe-shops, which means that people's minds are in shoes. **(In a serious tone)** It's the ugly deed that disgraces its doer and his folk… as for these simple clothes, they don't disgrace me… Besides, I like to free my feet, not to enchain them in soles …that I may walk freely everywhere...**(Joking)** and don't forget that the prices of shoes have risen to an unbearable point, so I'm sparing you all this… **(After a while)** Ah if only people would all walk bare-footed…nude… then they would know the truth

Xanthula: You're violating the nature of things and following what people aren't used to… these are festivities and celebrations, full of joy and glee...and…

Socrates: And what have new clothes and soles got to do with celebrations and glee?

Xanthula: These festivities are held for the gods who are-as you know-of beautiful countenance, loving for all that is beauty…so we have to meet them in new clothes and…

Socrates: **(Interrupting)** Rather say in new thought… **(Adding)** besides, the gods who can not accept me as I am… I will not accept them nor do I care for their festivities.

Xanthula: **(Raises her eyes and hands to the sky)** O! God Zeus, God of Gods forgive him… for he is a reckless philosopher! **(Adding)** Nothing spoils the mind like philosophy. **(Addressing Socrates)** You are insulting the Gods… you must ask for their forgiveness right now, otherwise they'll disgrace you. Children… **(Realizing the presence of the children and the maid… addresses Hedone)** why are you standing like that?... The children were not supposed to hear that talk... nor see their parents in this state **(A moment of pause)** take them to the bathroom…and I'll join you. **(Hedone and the children leave, as Xanthula approaches Socrates)** Huh, sweetie, ask for the Gods' pardon and all the problems of the universe will be solved.

Socrates: But I did nothing wrong… I ask you a definite question which is definitely unmistakably clear: do the gods wear soles?

Xanthula: It is a simple, clear and unmistakable question. Socrates, I don't know... to think of these matters is atheism. All I care for is to dress well.

Socrates: So at least it is possible that gods don't wear soles in their feet?

Xanthula: You're right…I think they wander in space and encircle around the skies bare-footed and nude…

Socrates: So I object… I refuse to go to meet the gods in the festivities in new clothes, and old or new soles…as long as they don't do that.

Xanthula: But these are Gods and we've got to accept them and meet them in any image. I believe in their presence, and I meet them whether with or without soles…this is the true belief… as for you, you've lost your mind... your rash will ruin us.

Socrates: Don't be nervous, calm down, so as not to spoil the dialogue.

Xanthula: But why don't you like meeting the gorgeous Gods in bright new clothes? Even Hera herself, queen of the sky, beautifies herself, wears the most beautiful ornaments when she is about to meet her beloved husband Zeus.

Socrates: She does that for other reasons that you know well. And I have a little question.

Xanthula: All your questions are terrifying… but I'll hear you anyway…this is my fate.

Socrates: I am what I am… am I not handsome?

Xanthula: You are handsome, Socrates? (**Laughs**) You are handsome, Socrates! (**Laughs**) Oh, how terrible! What has happened to your mind? Haven't you seen your face in the mirror?

Socrates: I only look in the reflection of myself from the inside…I don't care much for the outer appearance. I see my image in the reactions of others generally towards my behaviour and through my meditation of my true self.

Xanthula: And do you find yourself handsome?

Socrates: I'm trying to reach the highest degree of beauty.

Xanthula: And what cosmetics do you use?

Socrates: The soul does not use cosmetics and perfumes. I don't care for appearance; what concerns me is the essence. I think that those who beautify themselves with colors and perfumes are those who feel utter ugliness within… so they make up for it with false decoration on the outside.

Xanthula: (**Sharply**) Socrates… Socrates! What is it that you want to say exactly?

Socrates: Nothing …nothing.

Xanthula: Do you mean to tell me I'm ugly! Just say it out loud and don't be afraid, coward.

Socrates: You're right…you are the only person that makes me feel a coward, for you are stronger than me in tongue and hands…and feet. (**He moves away**) I'm scared of your kicking. (**Moves further**)

Xanthula: I am wrong. I, daughter of the elite, marrying you a scoundrel, when I had in front of me the most beautiful young men of the lineage in Athens…but for love…I was young, blinded by love and I couldn't see your ugliness...

Socrates: Any discussion with you is not safe… I am going out, I am leaving this house to you. (**About to leave when Xanthula stands in his way**)

Xanthula: No, you are not running away from me, this discussion must come to an end.

Socrates : (**Trying to go out**) Alright. Let me go out for a breath of fresh air and I'll be back.

Xanthula: Oh, no, never, you won't go out till we reach a solution…

Socrates: About what?

Xanthula: About our marital life…divorce me… (**She cries**)

Socrates: And why?

Xanthula: You said that whoever wears cosmetics and uses perfumes to beautify himself is ugly…and you know that I use them all the time…and all for you (**She cries**).

Socrates: If you're doing it all day long and doing nothing else, then you're very ugly indeed.

Xanthula: **(Nervously)** Shut up! **(Kicks a little table with a little jug full of hot water, it falls on Socrates who, in turn, falls on his face, the hot water pouring all over his body)**

Socrates: **(Flat on the floor moaning)** Oh, my broken bones…my scalded skin…damn you.

Xanthula: **(Kicking him)** Me ugly! You and your bald head shining in the dark and your flat nose giving out smoke like a chimney, giving out snores in your sleep like a ventilator.

Socrates: Leave me… Have mercy on me …I've got lectures, I want to go out… lend me your hand, help me get up and go.

Xanthula: No, I won't lend my hand to a petty insignificant like you. **(Chaerephon enters rushing, as he speaks in excitement)**

Chaerephon: Socrates, my friend Socrates, glad tidings, Socrates, the skies themselves have raised you up high, Socrates. **(He becomes aware that Socrates is on the floor)** But why are you lying down on your face like that? Are you united with the earth in search for its nature… your belly touching its core? So this must be a lesson in geology. **(Turning to Xanthula)** Is it you, lady, who drove him to this hard toil?

Xanthula: **(Turns away, saying)** You're as foolish as my husband! Aren't you friends…birds of the same feather, flock together. **(Talking to herself)** I'd better go bath my children.

Chaerephon: **(Approaching Socrates, patting his back)** Get up Socrates, don't worry …get up hero, your wife has gone.

Socrates : Leave me alone.

Chaerephon: Stop starring at the floor like this… one like you should be turning his sight to the stars in the sky…get up, keep your head up.

Socrates: I am worthless.

Chaerephon: Say something else, because the sky itself placed you higher than the rest of the humans.

Socrates: **(Gets up, still in a sitting position, saying sarcastically)** True! Who else would deserve such an untamed wife more than me…oh…!**(He hurts, touches parts of his body, tries to turn down once more on his face, Chaerephon stops him)**

Chaerephon: No…no…don't go back to that degrading position again. **(In an artificial tone)** You are the wisest of all creatures.

Socrates: **(Stands up impatiently)** Stop this sarcasm… this must be one of your silly allegations?

Chaerephon: But this is what the oracle said.

Socrates: This would never emit from gods.

Chaerephon: But didn't you hear of what happened?

Socrates: Alright…I'm listening.

Chaerephon: As soon as I went into the Apollo temple in Delphi, I found the Pythian priestess sitting on her tripod, the triangular chair, underneath which was a big pot of boiling water with fumes emitting out of it.

Socrates: **(Interrupting him, handling his body)** Boiling waters…oh my back!

Chaerephon: **(Continuing)** I wasted no time and immediately asked her a question, clearly, and smoothly. In brief I told her: is there anyone among humanity wiser than Socrates?

Socrates: **(Interrupting sharply)** This is a totally bad beginning, for you started with a pre-judgment as if it was taken for granted that Socrates is wise.

Chaerephon: **(Ignoring Socrates' words and continuing)** And when the priestess heard my question, she stretched out her hands, so when I gave her the silver piece of coin, she stretched out her other hand, so I put in it a piece of gold.

Socrates: **(Interrupting)** Even the oracles of gods don't come without bribes! Upon my word!

Chaerephon: **(Continuing)** Then, she muttered a few words and turned facing the three poets standing close to her… they became all ears expecting to grasp each big or little thing the priestess does, who kept shaking her head to and fro, back and forward, the shakings becoming stronger till she fell down on her face …falling into a stronger trance.

Socrates: **(Interrupting, terrified)** In boiling water…!?

Chaerephon: **(Ignoring Socrates' words)** And while the strange cosmic music was filling space, echoing everywhere, on top of the mountains, and deep in the valleys and woods, in different sounds; it started with strange noises I have never heard before, coming from the Pythian priestess, which may have been some sort of moaning or rattling… the important thing is that the priestess showed signs of deep fatigue followed by relaxation… cold sweat… long sighs… as a woman in labor… that I felt sorry for her and was about to take back the question that had exhausted her to that extent…

Socrates: I wish you hadn't asked it in the first place!

Chaerephon: What really provoked me is the behaviour of the three poets, who were like idiots: for the more tired Priestess was, the more they smiled and laughed. When the priestess was completely exhausted, they prepared to leave, rolling their sleeves and tongues, as though about to deliver an enthusiastic speech. And when the Priestess' murmurs turned into horrifying roaring screams, horrifying…other groups of priests and priestesses came out of everywhere in the temple… from sideway corridors, from the sacred sanctuary in the centre of the building… all beating the drums, singing and dancing…they gathered around me in a tight circle, took me to where I found myself outside the temple… for I was dizzy, unconscious of anything, and of all what was said, I couldn't hear anything clearly.

Socrates: So they kicked you out of the temple?

Chaerephon: No…they didn't kick me, but they congratulated me on proclaiming the oracle… asking me to wait a while to receive the formal text… For the three poets took to translating the unintelligible priestess' murmurs into intelligible and versed words.

Socrates: And why were the priestess' voices unintelligible?

Chaerephon: Because Apollo's spirit possessed her while she incarnated his character, speaking in his tongue.

Socrates: And Apollo's tongue does not utter the intelligible?

Chaerephon: Do you ask the immortal Gods to talk clearly and fluently like petty humans? (**Adding**) Socrates! Not everybody understands the words of heaven, only some of them can… And it is their duty to explain and interpret them for everybody.

Socrates: Alright.

Chaerephon: I spent three days and nights outside the temple… the three poets came on the dawn of the fourth day, and they recited to me a long hexameter poem… and, of course, I couldn't understand most of it…its content generally said "no one is wiser than Socrates" …and I congratulate you on this valuable confidence that Heaven has bestowed upon you, for fortune has opened its arms to you (**Tries to embrace Socrates, who avoids him**).

Socrates: You sure are an idiot, do you know what it means if this oracle is realized? It's an assignment rather than an honor, it'll put more responsibilities on my shoulders, more work, more thinking, more dialoguing and discussing… my wife won't give me a break…damn you, Chaerephon! Who told you to go to Delphi? O miserable me! **(Democratia, Chief of the State and elected demagogic leader, enters)**

Democratia: Greetings to Socrates wisest of the wise.

Socrates: You too, dignified chief, have heard of the catastrophic oracle? And do you believe it?

Democratia: **(Whispering to herself)** Even before it is proclaimed **(Raising her voice)** whoever undertakes the responsibility of the presidency has to proceed the incidents and compete with time. **(Coming closer to Socrates)** What matters now is that I congratulate myself and the state, before I congratulate you, Socrates.

Socrates: It is indeed an honor that Democratia, rational chief of our state is visiting us in our home, but I only want to inform her that I cannot believe this oracle.

Democratia: Believe it or not, that is a subordinate matter, what matters is that we believe…and your denial of the oracle shows your modesty, and ensures us further of your wisdom… for the more you reject it, the more we cling to it. (**She comes closer to Socrates, whispers in his ear**) Also, we invite you to cooperate with us.

Socrates: In what?

Democratia: In ruling.

Socrates: Me, cooperate with you…the government?

Democratia: Why not?

Socrates: For a thousand reasons.

Democratia: Anyway… I'll give you a chance to think it over…you mustn't rush matters…consider what I offered you till we meet again… and now I must go…for there's an urgent meeting with the military leaders to decide on matters of war…so good-bye Socrates (**She leaves**).

Chaerephon: Now what will you do, wisest of the wise?

Socrates: First, this matter of the oracle should submit to my method of examination and clarification.

Chaerephon: How?

Socrates: My starting point is to doubt its validity…then comes confirmation through meditation and dialogue.

Chaerephon: I don't understand?

Socrates: I'll challenge this oracle… I'll try to discover someone wiser than myself…I'll roam the streets of Athens to dialogue with everyone I come across…and how I wish I'd find someone wiser than myself to go to Delphi with a clear evidence.

Chaerephon: My friend, Socrates….do what you want, but I disagree with you, because you are going against the tide … everything calls you to happiness…here is the chance to achieve profits and success…and you're refusing it all… If I were in your shoes, I would immediately welcome to be a partner of Democratia in ruling.

Socrates: Because you're not Socrates (**Socrates' students voices are heard outside**)

Voice 1: Our professor…Socrates.

Voice 2: Come out to us, professor.

Voice 3: Why are you late today, without you we can't live.

Voice 4: We are afraid to come in…you come out….

Chaerephon: Your students are waiting for you, Socrates.

Voice 5: You missed the lesson, professor.

Socrates: (**Talking to Chaerephon**) I'm not going out today…I'm pessimistic…scared.

Voice 1: Answer us, professor.

Voice 3: This is the first time you stay home all day.

Voice 4: We're worried that something may have happened to you.

All Voices: Come on, Socrates…we're not leaving till you come out.

Chaerephon: No room for hesitation… no way but to go out.

Socrates: I think my wife is standing by the door…I'm afraid there'll be a fight.

Chaerephon: Let's jump out of the back window…come on.

Socrates: I'm afraid I'll fall and break my bones.

Chaerephon: You'll break your bones in both cases… come, I'll help you **(Takes his hand and helps him to jump out of the back window… shortly, the shouts of the students are heard… the wife runs through the house looking for Socrates, but doesn't find him… she goes to the window, out of which he jumped… sees Socrates with his students around him**).

Xanthula: Socrates… come back home, Socrates. Your young children are more important than these parasitical worms. (**Pointing to Athenian youth, Socrates' students**) Socrates, you'll regret that… is this how you keep yourself busy in conversation, so as not to answer me… (**She calls loudly**) Hedone, quickly Hedone (**Hedone comes, carrying a big container full of water**) Then take Socrates and your students, this dirty water which my children bathed in, and which is cleaner than your ugly faces gypsies…huh. (**The youth gather around Socrates who is bare-footed and draw back slowly, as somebody throws a pair of shoes from Socrates' house, making noises when they hit the ground behind Socrates and his students**).

Scene II

The Price of Freedom

(In this scene, both the stage and the auditorium form the agora-the public meeting place of Athens, where Socrates and his students are roaming. At the right end of the auditorium stands the Maker of gods' statues. On the left hand-side of the auditorium, Ion, the epic poet, will appear and sit, surrounded by part of the audience. On the stage, there is a platform where Democratia will stand to deliver a political speech. The auditorium and the platform may be lit up simultaneously at the beginning of the scene, and then darkened again, so that spot-lightning could be shed successively on the different participants in the dialogues).

Socrates: Good morning, immortal Maker of gods' statues.

Maker of gods' statues: Good morning, wise Socrates.

Socrates: You are a skilful artist…. Maker of the most wonderful gods' statues in Athens… how are you? And is your merchandise still prospering?

Maker of gods' statues: Well… thank gods anyway… (**Sighing**) people don't believe in gods anymore like in the old times, but they go on buying statues to decorate their houses and vehicles,… and temples, as is their habit or inherited customs.

Socrates: Your very presence is proof of the people's keenness to strengthen good relationships with the immortal gods.

Maker of gods' statues: That's true.

Socrates: So your craft is participating in keeping the old religious beliefs and traditions.

Maker of gods' statues: That's also true.

Socrates: I also experienced this occupation for a long time, for I had inherited it from my ancestors.

Maker of gods' statues: And you left it.

Socrates: Yes.

Maker of gods' statues: And how could you dare to leave what you inherited from your ancestors? Was it not profitable?

Socrates: On the contrary, it is the most profitable of crafts, like shoe cobbling, you know this very well… aren't you among the richest people in the city? Both you and the cobblers?

Maker of gods' statues: Then why did you leave it?

Socrates: Money, profit is not the best aim in life.

Maker of gods' statues: I don't understand you, Socrates. For how can you differentiate between profit and highest good in this life?

Socrates: I'm searching for a craft that would build souls and teach wisdom.

Maker of gods' statues: And I can only know the craft that bears profit, for the more my profits increase, the more I know my craft, know its secrets, till I master it completely.

Socrates: This is quite clear to you, for no one surpasses you in the making of Olympian gods' statues.

Maker of gods' statues: Because I make the highest profits among sculptors.

Socrates: But haven't you thought one day to make other useful functions out of this craft?

Maker of gods' statues: You are really strange, Socrates, for I am the one who beautifies the gods' temples with the most beautiful statues… besides, were it not for the skill of my hands, our temples wouldn't have been as beautiful and probably people would have deserted them.

Socrates: I didn't mean that.

Maker of gods' statues: **(Continuing)** It is I who raised the standard of artistic taste for most of the people. Suffice for them to lay their eyes every day on my own statues, for they are masterpieces of creative art.

Socrates: This is what I'm thinking of, for I am going deeper than that, and more precisely I want to ask you if you have meditated about this craft of yours?

Maker of gods' statues: How?

Socrates: Why are you making statues of Gods?

Maker of gods' statues: For the people to see.

Socrates: You mean if people didn't see these statues, they wouldn't worship the gods?

Maker of gods' statues: I guess so.

Socrates: And have you seen the gods?

Maker of gods' statues: No… but then who sees them?

Socrates: Alright… So how did you imagine them in these images? Here you are carving the statue of the Zeus, the god of gods, as a strong man holding a scepter and thunderbolt in his hand, close to him stands the hawk **(Pointing to Zeus's statue)**; and Poseidon in the shape of a man holding the trident, the three ended scepter **(Pointing to the statue of Poseidon)**; and Dionysus waving with a twig branch and grape-vines **(Pointing to the statue of Dionysus)**. In the name of these gods, how did you recognize each of their figures?

Maker of gods' statues: This is what traditional tales and stories told us, and information we inherited from our own forefathers.

Socrates: Is it a must, to follow whatever inherited from fathers and fore-fathers?

Maker of gods' statues: Tell me, you, how would you draw the gods?

Socrates: I don't know! For I, like you, haven't seen the gods… but I don't draw them or imagine them. For looking into the matter of the presence, of these gods, their natures is longer or larger than our mortal human span of life, for the years of life are all too short, and don't allow a prolonged looking into the matter, and so I am really surprised when I see a maker of gods' statues, picturing them in human forms!

Maker of gods' statues: And is there a more beautiful and perfect form than that of man among all creatures?

Socrates: Of course not.

Maker of gods' statues: No wonder then that humans picture their gods in this beautiful form…

Socrates: True…but accordingly… every species in creation has a right to admire its form and picture its gods as such.

Maker of gods' statues: This is a mystery I can't understand.

Socrates: **(Adding)** If the animalistic species held the carving instruments to draw the gods…they would draw them in the form of animals… for it is impossible according to what you say that animals draw their gods in human form…for this would mean that oxen worship oxen…donkeys draw donkeys to worship…and so on… Of course this is just an imaginary assumption….but it may help us to refuse... the current image of deities in human form…

Maker of gods' statues: And in what picture do you imagine them, Socrates?

Socrates: I told you several times I don't know…but why can't gods be present in everything…in the sky, in the bottom of the earth, bottom of seas, top of the mountains, in space, in air, in water and fire…huh, why not?

Maker of gods' statues: You mean they assume all shapes… don't settle with any certain form… and that it is everywhere.

Socrates: Exactly… they are in everything; they are nothing definite and exclusively.

Maker of gods' statues: So how can we carve the statues then?

Socrates: Worshipping gods needs no statues.

Maker of gods' statues: And the temples, how do we decorate them?

Socrates: No need for temples…if we worship gods in our own hearts…then all of nature is the best temple for gods.

Maker of gods' statues: And so you intend to destroy us… How, then, can we find our own bread?

Socrates: I don't care…common good is what interests me, everything else is false.

Maker of gods' statues: Scram from my face then, or I'll break your head **(Waves with the carving knife, but Socrates' students rush and gather around Socrates, defending him, pulling him slowly away)**.

Socrates: Don't be afraid, my students, for this idiot can't hurt me…he is weaker and worse. So how can he get me, the stronger and the better? See how he resorts to violence? This violence is proof of weakness…for the quiet word is the sword of the intellectual. He collapsed before my words…he knows nothing, not even about his own craft of which he claims he masters—he harms society, the gods…also himself, out of his stupidity.

Maker of gods' statues: You mistakable, lazy good- for nothing: you want us to denounce the deities we inherited from our own fore-fathers? Or perhaps you wish for us to do nothing like yourself… to become roisters? (**Pointing to the students**) Take him away… or I'll break his empty head… It's bald, looks like a broken balloon, how I feel like banging it with my chisel (**Tries to come closer to Socrates, his students taking him further, going slowly towards the opposite side of the agora; there, they find Ion busy singing and playing music as fans and the public surround him**).

Ion (Singing)

Sing for me goddess of poverty

With magical words

Sing for these noblemen

Of the valiant hero

Of Odysseus the wanderer who

Forsook his homeland and island

For twenty years

And the greedy princes

Wanted to

Make his wife forget

The meaning of faithfulness and longing.

They told her:

"Odysseus is dead".

But, gentlemen

Lest we are taken into words

I should like to ask you in amity

Of what you wish to listen to today

Of Odysseus' story

And his very faithful

Wife Penelopia

Who ruled the country and the folk

With loyalty

Penelopia is a symbol of faithfulness.

A listener's Voice: Tell us his story with the witch that turned his friends into pigs…the unscrupulous.

Voice 2: I'm not too fond of listening to the faithful wife Penelope…the smart.

Voice 3: Perhaps it is best to leave the choice to Ion, for he knows the secrets in Odysseus' home…his adventures in the seas…you choose, Ion… choose.

Ion: I choose? Goddesses of arts will choose and send me the inspiration from the top of the mountains, with the rustle of leaves…and I…

Socrates: **(Interrupting)** Listen Ion, you are a fantastic poet and this ancient epic song is witness of your craft… but I have a few questions …

Voice 3: At this time?

Voice 1: It is silliness.

Voice 2: Leave us now, Socrates, we don't need you, here is a serious man singing from heritage, they are not light songs of today.

Socrates: Comrades, dear sons of Athens, I don't wish to spoil your pleasure…for I too love the folkloric heritage of songs, but…

Voice 1: **(Interrupting)** You mean, we don't understand what we hear?

Voice 2: Now that Socrates started by "but", his speech will never end… **(Addressing Socrates)** Socrates, we neither want to listen, nor to understand words of philosophers.

Voice 3: Leave us alone, Socrates. **(To Ion)** Sing, Ion.

Ion: I told you a thousand times I don't sing, it's the goddess of poetry who sings through my tongue…I am her tongue.

Socrates : **(Interrupting)** I like your modesty Ion, but…

Voice 2: "But" again…oh cursed day!

Socrates: **(Ignoring and adding)** I noticed once that you mentioned the goddess of poetry, and another time "goddesses" so which is the right one…singular or plural?

Ion: I don't know… I utter whatever comes to me by inspiration…

Socrates: All right… I know you don't utter through your own desire…

A voice interrupting: And what has desire got to do here?

Socrates: **(Adding)**… but from the first couplet you are saying "sing", so are you using the imperative with the gods? I also noticed that you are switching Penelope's name to Penelopia…

Ion: As to the last point: this is part of the craft… for after the inspired superior chief Democratia ruled the country, I have since been singing in the name of Odysseus' wife as Penelopaia, as to make it close to the name of Democratia. And like that I employed heritage in the service of the present and the future. Do you think that we are playing around, sir! Isn't every thing dandy!

Socrates: Well done, well done.

Ion: **(Adding)** As to the foreword: "sing" this is your ailment … the imperative here means begging and pleading, there is something in it of an intimacy… sing me a little.

Socrates: So some words carry an apparent meaning, others are hidden in the mind of the poet…isn't it so?

Ion: Maybe so.

Socrates: You are of all people supposed to be qualified to understand Homer, being a singer of his verses?

Ion: I guess so.

Socrates: And when Homer describes the battles of Troy as an expert of war, does this imply that he had a great knowledge of war?

Ion: Yes, nobody can describe battles better than Homer.

Socrates: It seems he's an experienced cunning military leader?

Ion: No, he's nearer to the war hero himself Achilles… or to Democratia, superior chief of our country, who cancelled the word defeat from our dictionary, for all her steps are victories, all her decisions are historical and inspired, for she is the heroine of war and peace.

Socrates: Never mind this now, I'm talking about Homer and I ask you simply: do you know what Homer knows?

Ion: Of course.

Socrates: So why beg a goddess or goddesses of poetry?

Ion: They inspire our songs and meanings too.

Socrates: You don't understand what you're singing without them?

Ion: Yes.

Socrates: This applies to Homer?

Ion: Of course.

Socrates: So Homer doesn't know the arts of war?

Ion: Yes … he doesn't.

Socrates: And you are singing his verses without understanding them?

Ion: That's right.

Socrates: So you're only a deaf machine without the goddess of poetry…or rather you are a parrot?

Ion: Exactly…I'm a parrot... a stupid… I'm a parrot! ...but how come I never knew that before?

Socrates: (Addressing the audience in the hall) And if that singer is a parrot repeating only what he hears unconsciously then you, people, will be even more stupid if you surround him again. You should free yourself of this rotten singer and his backward songs that spoil your tastes and cause retardation.

Voice 1: Socrates, you are rude, for you are attacking us.

Voice 2: And you are a coward, Ion, for succumbing to that arrogant philosopher.

Voice 3: Courage, Ion, throw a hot poem in his ugly face.

Ion: **(Singing together with the audience)**:

Philosopher of desolation

Let us be
O most illustrous
O most learned
Your words and judgments
Are worth less than a surplus nail.
Whoever is present, tell the absent
To throw away damned Socrates
On heaps of garbage
Miserable philosopher
Let us be
O most illustrous
O most learned
Your words and judgments
Are not even worth a cut-off nail

Voice 1: Scram! Socrates.

Voice2: Scram or we'll kill you.

Voice 3: You spoilt our fun, we missed our view, damn you! ... **(The three listeners walk towards Socrates; his students surround him, defending him, pulling him away from Ion, seating him in the middle of the hall in the front row, as the light focuses on the stage platform where behind the panel of the speaker stands the demagogic Democratia)**.

Democratia: **(Speaking)** My dear people, sons of a thousand-temple Athens, holders of glory, builders of a civilization of thousands of years, I have gathered you today, because I never act without your consent, our nation is a nation of consultation, he who consults the people never fails in matters of rule. You are the beginning and end in every decision I make. We live in a democratic country…our city of ancient Athens is the school of democracy…it has taught Greece, may be the whole world, to draft the constitution and the principle of respect for the laws and equality among citizens, grandchildren of Solon and sons of Pericles… Athens is the castle of freedom, the oasis of security… the sanctuary of every free man of the Hellenic nation, from the Ocean to the Saronic Gulf ...the area surrounding us is boiling in wars and schemes... disruptions, and here you are enjoying tranquility, peace of mind and prosperity…all this we owe to freedom and Democracy. (**Sharp applause**) O citizens, free Athenians! In the name of you all I send my greetings to the front…to those who are fighting a war of honor in face of the Spartan enemy…my children on the front are fighting day and night, while you are sleeping in deep slumber. Those are my children who have raised the banner of honor, when they overcame the rebellions in the Greek islands… in Lesbos, Euboea, and Melos and others... and it is my children who are now standing in a row facing the Spartan extending march…and Sparta as you know is a totalitarian country, where everything and everyone surrenders to the one ruler… Man in Sparta is but a clog in a machine… helpless… Sparta is the enemy of freedom… Sparta must be destroyed. Yes, Sparta should be destroyed… and in your name I declare war on Sparta in land and sea till victory (**Sharp applause**).

Strong cries from the hall: Down with Sparta … down with Sparta, long live Athens free… long live Athens free, war! War! Till victory, blood and soul we die for you superior chief, long live Democratia, long live Democratia.

Democratia: Great people of Athens, sons of ancient civilization…free citizens…before I came to you here I passed a decree that entrance to the theatre for every citizen is free, young or old, rich or poor, with sight or blind…all are equal.

Applause from the hall: Long live Democratia…hail justice…hail justice...

Democratia: I have also decided to offer extra rations to ensure that these materials may reach those who deserve them, and not to leak to the black market, I have decided to divide citizens into three categories: that of the poor, to receive red ostraca and all ration materials for free, including olive oil, wine, and meat…as to the second category, of limited incomes, those are to receive yellow ostraca, they pay half prices of whatever they take. As to the third category, of the well-off, these receive white ostraca, they have the right to the basic rations, only wine for I know that none of them can do without that sort…it is important you do not confuse ration with election ostraca. (**She pauses**) And speaking of the coming elections, I promise they will be a hundred percent clean, I myself will supervise them, there will be no forgery. You know that the past elections were all fake. I witnessed the forging myself: they put a bottomless container over a deep hole in the sand and you come and mark your vote on the ostraca and then throw them in this container and like this your votes drop into the earth's bottom. At the close of the elections, they would lift the bottomless container, your votes having been buried in the sands, and bring another one with a bottom full of forged election ostraca; the result of the elections would appear, announcing that famous three or five nines…and this is how they forged the will of the people…but this time… there will be no forgery.

Socrates: (**Rises and intrudes**) Does this mean that you yourself came to the rule by forged elections?

Deomcratia: (**Nervous, sweating, wipes her forehead with a handkerchief, ignoring Socrates' words, staggers**) My dear people, you are the best to defend democracy from her enemies. (**Pulling herself together**) …and the coming elections will be clean… completely.

Socrates: He who lacks cannot give, superior chief.

Democratia: Socrates, you of all people can't speak about Democracy.

Socrates: Why?

Democratia: Because you allied with the enemies of Democracy. The government of the thirty that displaced thousands and imprisoned thousands…it spared none of the democrats in the city... while you enjoyed peace in this damned government for your beloved student Alcibiades, one of the chiefs of this rotten lot patronized you and…

Socrates: (**Interrupting**) First of all, I have not left Athens during the rule of this despotic government because I don't like to leave Athens whatever the circumstances. I don't leave my motherland and my birthplace willingly, unless the city itself entrusts me with a patriotic mission outside the borders.

Democratia: Haven't you allied with this government?

Socrates: It has been proved beyond doubt that I have violated this government's orders, when it wished to send me with four others to arrest a citizen, to sentence him to death. I left them and stayed at home, I almost lost my life, hadn't that government fell… as for me I am not an enemy to Democracy… those who ruin Democracy are those who forge elections and deceive the people.

Democratia: If you are accusing me of forgery and deceit, I shall let the people judge.

Socrates: I know how you bring the poor people's satisfaction by the slightest remnants of your luxurious banquets, you give them some oil, and wheat, and wine...while you and your relatives exploit the state's possessions and monopolize some of the concessions like arms, land, and commerce in agricultural products, and local industrial and imported products. You invest your money at the expense of the people's food; sometimes you even import rotten food.

Democratia: There is nothing in our constitution that prohibits commerce, for it is allowed for the ruler and the ruled alike.

Socrates: But the commerce that depends on the political status of its owner…is no commerce, but rather comes under the job-abuse and illegal earnings.

Democratia: **(Descends the podium, approaches Socrates)** Does this mean that in your opinion the ruler must be poor?

Socrates: If he is fair and not greedy, he will find wealth in his peoples' contentment and in their love for him.

Democratia: **(Approaching Socrates, whispers in his ear)** This is philosophers' talk that can never be practical. **(Stretching out her hand)** Come, Socrates … didn't I tell you before that we can cooperate... come, Socrates, that we may reach an understanding **(He moves away from her… she withdraws her hand and goes back to her place on the podium)** Socrates, don't forget that elections are coming and that we are in a state of war, and I will not allow one creature, whoever he is, to implant the seeds of mutiny among the people.

Socrates: And this war is another crime, for Sparta, on which you have declared war, is a neighboring state… there is no need for this war. It shows great stupidity: for instead of uniting the Hellenic nation to confront the main and everlasting enemy, which is the Persian empire, we squander our efforts in an endless war with our Spartan neighbors, for no reason, except that their political system differs from ours.

Democratia: War is imposed upon us because Sparta is competing with us in leadership, thus turning their cities and islands against us. Also, it has rejected the charter of Delos treaty.

Socrates: It was necessary to make an agreement with the Spartans to face the Persians who are expanding in the minor and neighboring islands at the expense of the Hellenic nation. Did you forget the Persian enclosure of the resistance fighters in Smyrna? That city held on for several months and when it failed to find help since its call for help was not heard by the neighbors who were involved in their home differences, its heroic fighters abandoned the city and fled to Ephesus. Ephesus itself was later oppressed by the arrogant Persian enemy and so the heroic resistance was broken into pieces for a second time. All this was taking place while the Hellen was fighting the Hellen… the Athenian attacking the Spartan while the Persian enemy is roistering in the area.

Democratia: And is this my fault?

Socrates: You are to blame for all that…for because of the war with Sparta, its flames spread to the Saronic Gulf…kindling the war between Corinth and Megara…and this gulf war will never stop until it destroys the two states completely, for the citizens of each of them are known to be fierce in their combating. I wonder how two states could fight, whose people worship the same gods and speak one language?

Democratia: And you are blaming me for all this?

Socrates: Because you mislead the people and cheat them with your sweet talk… you promised them prosperity… but you never carry out your promise… for in war there cannot be any prosperity. You claimed to establish democracy and to support its pillars, while you are head-strong, you forge the elections, you are like the malignant malady that destroys the body, even before a person can feel it…

Democratia: But it's you who are deluded, you philosopher of nonsense…searching for things that don't exist on earth…contemplating on air and space…walking on earth unconsciously…neglecting worldly matters **(Going on)** all people support me with their love…they know that you're good for nothing…could you lead a nation?

Socrates: Me? Of course not, and I am aware of that and I admit it too.

Democratia: And why?

Socrates: Because I don't know lying and deceit, acting, flattering, changing faces and maneuvering. I, Democratia, seek to reach the truth by the shortest way, that is through a straight line… but for you and other politicians, all lines are wavering and crooked, interconnected and interwoven, even changeable and fickle… sometimes you can't even find a single line.

Democratia: So you denounce our political life.

Socrates: Yes…and I particularly deplore demagoguism.

Democratia: And you're no good for it.

Socrates: Nor is it for me.

Democratia: But in this way you stand out as an onlooker, criticizing things from the outside…where you should be on the inside…

Socrates: What do you mean?

Democratia: To stand for the next elections with us. (**Addressing the hall**) What do you say my dear people?

Voice 1: Whatever you say, our dear inspired leader.

Voice 2: If you can see some use for politics in that man… we'll back him up, if you wish.

Voice 3: Only don't rush it, superior chief, for you can't trust those people, for an educated hypocrite is a thousand times more dangerous than any other hypocrite.

Socrates: (**Ignoring the hall**) Me, standing for elections! (**Laughs**)

Democratia: And why not?

Socrates: (**Pointing to the hall**) None of those will vote for me… for they know my ugly face… for I am neither among those famous, whom other people like to befriend, nor am I the rich one of those people who seek their friendship, nor am I the hypocrite who shuts an eye to peoples' shortcomings, nor am I the eloquent rhetorician who toys with peoples' hearts by his eloquence, touching their very souls…

Democratia: Never mind all this…we guarantee your means to success; all that we ask of you is to write your name in the list of our candidates.

Socrates: But…who is that genius who created the system of election by list? He has surpassed even Pythagoras! Indeed the Hellenis soil is fertile!

Democratia: We are not discussing now the election system… and answer my question… are you with us?

Socrates: I'll tell you a funny story about Aristides the Just who, ruled Athens during the sound democratic age.

Democratia: **(Bored)** This is not the time.

Socrates: **(Ignoring her)** A member of the Assembly presented to one of his envious adversaries a draft involving the banishment of Aristides from Athens… and when Aristides went to the Assembly to vote… the security guard, distributing the election ostraca, mistook him for an ordinary citizen…so he handed him the ostracon whispering: write "I agree"… so when Aristides asked him "why do you want to banish Aristides?" The guard answered "because he is no longer just". Aristides carried out the guard's wish, voted on the proposal in the affirmative… thus participating himself by his vote, in his own banishment…in favor of democracy and justice, saying as he bid farewell to Athens on his way to the exile" I can't understand how a ruler could sit on his seat knowing that someone is complaining of his injustice?!"

Democratia: Then try and later do what Aristides did.

Socrates: No… because the glamour of the throne of authority is quite tempting… I may sit on it and become blind to the truth, not knowing when to quit. And since I know I'm not fit to practice politics and authority…so why put myself in a place incompatible with my tendencies?

Democratia: Alright, so only be my cultural consultant… supervise matters of arts, literature and philosophy… for you are the wisest of all.

Socrates: I'm still in the stage of skepticism of the Delphi's oracle carried by Chaerephon and it follows that I'm not the wisest of the wise…nor am I the best one who can understand cultural matters in the city. Likewise, on the other hand, I don't find you the best, or that you're better than anyone else, or that you've got a claim to the throne.

Democratia: But I'm actually ruling.

Socrates: And that's the catastrophe.

Democratia: And I myself will stand for elections to carry on the rule.

Socrates: Then there is no hope.

Democratia: And I'm sure that all sectors of society support me and surround me with their love.

Socrates: Stupidity is like a fever, doesn't stop when one individual is catching it, but rather it hits a whole nation, for it is a destructive epidemic.

Democratia: My beloved people…here you are …witnessing Socrates and listening to him as he addresses me with the meanest of insults and swears at you and your democratic regime… all his plans have been fully uncovered, and within the context of the democratic regime, I leave him to you…the people will be the best judge …so decide what you will.

Voice 1: Hit him with your golden sole, o leader.

Voice 2: Send him to prison, O just ruler.

Voice 3: As long as we kick him out of this sacred place…out, out Socrates.

(The hall roars with cries).

Out, out Socrates, go to the streets, wander… be a vagrant you bare-footed…do what you will, out…out Socrates (**Socrates leaves, surrounded by his students, the curtain falls**).

Scene III

Towards a Clean Environment

(Same scene as the first; a few aspects of festivities are added, like flames and candles, laurel branches; time is before dawn, an atmosphere of expectation hovers)

Hedone: Milady Xanthula, you haven't slept a wink that night… are you worried over Socrates who hasn't returned till now?

Xanthula: No, I've got used to that… I can't even tell the difference if he's here or if he is absent out of the house. He comes and goes any time… philosophy has taken him completely away from me. I just worry lest it be the withering of my beauty to be the cause of his repulsion from home.

Hedone: Milady… I have never seen anyone on earth more beautiful than you and if it were up to me I'd place you upon the throne of Aphrodite, the goddess of beauty herself…

Xanthula: **(Starring in a mirror in her hand)** Don't be too flattering.

Hedone: But it is true…it's what I do believe…no one on earth is more beautiful than you are… and I am perfectly ready to go to Delphi's oracle…ask the god Apollo one definite question: is there anyone among the women of the earth more beautiful than sweet Xanthula?...I'm sure that the answer will definitely be negative.

Xanthula: So you are about to play the role of Chaerephon when he brought a similar oracle to Socrates? When the latter didn't believe it, he started to search for a man wiser than himself among painters, poets, and all intellectuals. And so, some scorned him, others ridiculed him, he ended up in something like madness. So, this is the destiny you wish for me?

Hedone: **(Serious and decisive)** But you aren't like your husband Socrates…god forbid…milady, for he is, to tell you the truth, the ugliest man in the world…and you are the most beautiful woman on earth. I really can't see how you accepted him as a husband.

Xanthula: Hedone, watch your tongue, be gentle in your frankness …at least in my presence…

Hedone: You got to prove this with real experience… and actual practice.

Xanthula: I don't understand anything.

Hedone: And I can't explain further. (**After a while**) I mean you have got to ask all the men in Athens if, and I am ready to help you in this mission, there is a sweeter, more beautiful woman than you (**Laughs cunningly**).

Xanthula: (**Smiling**) Enough! Be serious. **(Gazes in the mirror examining her features and combing her hair)** The wine of the Dionysiac festivities seems to take away your mind.

Hedone: **(Whispers as though talking to herself)** Indeed these noisy festivities held for this vagrant god are about to get us. (**Shakes her waist**) What fun it is to dance in your feasts, o glorious god of wine… there, in the depth of the thick forest… in the company of drunken youth… after midnight as the drums beat around us… moving our hearts… hugging the branches… the grape vines dangling close to our mouths… the gentle breeze toying with our hair locks, all decorated with wreaths of twigs. In nights like those passions kindle… (**With rapture**) Oh… how beautiful life is! (**She becomes aware of her mistress**) Milady… the most beautiful woman in the world… my heart breaks for you as you live like this, imprisoned in this cage, underneath this ceiling.

Xanthula: Even you, Hedone, don't you like our way of life?

Hedone: Milady… you deserve the company of Dionysus and his crazy followers… how beautiful you are in the prime of youth and freshness of beauty… you could dance with Dionysus himself. (**Meditates for a second**) Beautify yourself, milady… beautify yourself for the fun festivities are soon to come… a celebration of joy and frivolity (**Socrates and his students enter silently, dragging their feet in silence, looking up as if staring at something; they seem as if amazed or distracted, unaware of their surroundings, now and then one of them looks at the other, goes back to contemplation; at first they are unnoticed by Hedone and Xanthula**).

Xanthula: This year in particular, I don't know why I'm curiously looking forward to attending the celebrations and following up the comic plays… something in them attracts me… maybe it's because I haven't laughed for some time heartily… and maybe…

Hedone: **(Interrupting)** It's because a new poet is presenting a new play.

Xanthula: Exactly… it's Aristophanes, who is said to have composed a play entitled *"Clouds"...*

Hedone: *"Clouds"...*

Xanthula: They said nothing about its subject, but the very name of the play attracts me very much.

Hedone: Anyway, the theatre was made for the free… we, the slaves are not allowed to follow up and even if they should allow us… I personally will not go to the theatre… I prefer the dance circles with drunken young people…

Xanthula: **(Interrupting her)** In the woods… after midnight… huh!

Hedone: **(Going on)** They're the faithful followers of Dionysus… oh milady, if only you would come with us… one night… one night will do… it'll make you forget the theatre and art... and everything... **(Swaying)** …is there anything better than roistering in the warm arms of Dionysus, in the company of his nice followers… **(Sweetly)** One night will suffice, milady.

Xanthula: Mind your manners, Hedone. **(After a while)** I've bought all these clothes… decorated myself in the best way surely not for your roisterer friends in the Dionysiac circle dance, but to attend the theatrical performances. This purple cloak made in Phoenician tyre - how much it cost! And this necklace, and these golden earrings… brought from the treasures of Ancient Egypt…and this wreath that I bought from Asian merchants, as for these shoes, they are made of the finest Arabic gazelle leather.

Hedone: And your husband… will you be taking him along to the theatre?

Xanthula: I know what you mean… I have already bought him fancy clothes… and I'll do my best to make him wear them.

Hedone: And will he give up his shabby rags? **(After a while)** And have you bought him shoes?

Xanthula: Of course.

Hedone: My master Socrates… will put shoes in his feet?! This is the feast of feasts. **(Pause)** He won't even know how to walk in them through the streets.

Xanthula: At first he'll walk with difficulty… but I don't believe he'll need a coach.

Hedone: Oh, but it's you who needs the assistance of the Olympus gods all together to make your husband wear shoes in his feet... willingly... then walk in them through the streets... it's such a difficult task! (**She realizes the presence of Socrates and his students**) But here is my master Socrates surrounded by a few of his insects... I mean a line of beetles.

Xanthula: (**Approaching Socrates**) At last you're here, Socrates... you haven't had a bite since yesterday. (**Socrates and his students still staring upward; from time to time some of them are bending their heads, almost touching the ground with their crowns**).

Hedone: (**Hiding behind Xanthula**) Milady, I'm scared!

Xanthula: Why, my girl?

Hedone: Their looks... wandering, staring, and looking fixedly at things.

Xanthula: But they are not looking at you...

Hedone: And their dangling long hair on their shoulders... full of fleas, they're polluting the environment wherever they go! As for their yellow faces... they remind me of damned death itself waiting for people all the time.

Xanthula: Leave them alone... they're pathetic, they break my heart.

Hedone: Why, milady?

Xanthula: They're thinking day and night like that (**pointing at them**) and when they are steeped in meditation they become as if in a state of labor or about to give birth now; and when engaged in a certain idea... they look into it thoroughly.

Hedone: And how do they look into it thoroughly?

Xanthula: Searching... and in that case they feel nothing around them... for they are in another world.

Hedone: So they're not with us now?

Xanthula: Exactly.

Hedone: So we can talk freely?!

Xanthula: At your ease.

Hedone: (**Slapping one of the students at the back of his neck**) Frankly, I despise them... and all ideas that distract a person from everything around him especially if it's a beautiful woman. **(She beautifies)** A man with a beautiful woman beside him and he meditates… definitely one of the two is mad!

Xanthula: The man of course… **(pauses)**. For me… it was my fate to live with one who knows nothing in the world but to meditate… but I got used to that. For despair is one of the two peaces. **(Sighs)** I've given him up. To me, he is non-existent in my life. **(Pointing at him)** As you can see, is this creature here at all?!

Hedone: **(Whispering)** Your sad lot!

Xanthula: **(Approaching Socrates, shaking him trying to get him out of his meditations)** …no way…no way. **(She stops in despair)** They're stuck in their place.

Hedone: Milady… why are they staring upward like that, open-mouthed?

Xanthula: Waiting for the heavens to pour ideas over them…

Hedone: But this ceiling only pours insects' waste… **(To herself)** Oh my poor lot… my colleagues are working in houses full of robust youth… healthy, beautiful… but these… they're hopeless… their very sight is disgusting.

Xanthula: What are you saying?

Hedone: Nothing… but what are you going to do now… we need an insecticide. **(Sighs)** We're all dressed up for the festivities!... Then the comrades came in… as if drunk… but not really drunk… And myself, I would like them indeed drunk!

Xanthula: I've got an idea.

Hedone: Out with it…

Xanthula: You know the pot we put on the fire, full of water?

Hedone: Yes.

Xanthula: Bring it… we'll pour it over their heads to bring them out of their meditation **(Hedone goes immediately and comes back with the pot, starts to pour the hot water over Socrates and his students' heads; they come about slowly).**

Socrates: **(Half alert)**…come on, it is raining, comrades… though I see no clouds. **(Stares in the air)** It's a rare phenomenon worthy of investigation… rain without clouds (**His students surrounding in a semi circle, raising their eyes upward**).

Xanthula: (**Piercing the circle, grabbing Socrates**) Awaken, Socrates… wake up (**shaking him violently**).

Socrates: (**Turning to his students**) Where are we, boys? (**He notices his wife**) What brings us to the underworld?! I can see Tartarus and the hell partners...

Xanthula: (**Shaking him**) You must wake up, Socrates… you're home. (**Leaves Socrates and returns threatening towards his students**) As for you, beetle shits… there's no place for you in our home… have you no families? Go home… scram! (**They don't move**) Hedone…Hedone…

Hedone: At your service, milady.

Xanthula: Give me the prick and the whip so that I can kick out these insects, right out of all the area… protecting the environment is a patriotic mission.

Hedone: Immediately, milady… (**Before she moves**) Though I'd rather you use on them rat poison or any other insecticide, for they'll spread the epidemic wherever they go, better get rid of them once and for all. (**She goes and comes back quickly, with the prick and whip; gives her mistress the whip, keeps the needle**).

Xanthula: (**Whipping one of the students on his feet**) Come on… scram of my face. (**The student turns around terrified as Hedone pricks him above his feet from the back. He screams and runs quickly outside; the same with the rest of the students**).

Xanthula: (**Exhausted, addressing Socrates who hasn't yet fully recovered his senses**) Sweetie… Socrates… Socrataki... come back to your wife. (**He still stares in the air**) You must awaken Socrates… I have something important to tell you… (**She pauses reflecting a little**) Hedone…Hedone.

Hedone: At your service, milady… you want me to prick him in his bald head?

Xanthula: No…No…quickly bring me some water.

Hedone: The prick is better.

Xanthula: **(Throwing the whip on the floor)** You stupid! As long as your master doesn't wake up, this is a golden opportunity… let him sleep as he is …we'll wash, dress him, and fix him up in new clothes and shoes as we wish. Then, I'll take him along with me to the theatre… the performance will start shortly.

Hedone: Wonderful idea… **(Soon adding)** But how will you take him to the theatre, while he is still floating in his meditations? He'll understand nothing.

Xanthula: It isn't important… do you think we go to the theatre for him to understand… no, we walk… we, the spectators, watch each other… notice each other's fashion, in clothes or in manners… we exchange talks and pistachio for entertainment… The theatre, Hedone, is a social gathering for the spectators' celebration that… **(After a pause)** Go… go get the water… **(She goes, returns immediately with water and basin; Xanthula holds Socrates' head, washes it as Hedone pours water)**.

Socrates : **(Slowly recovering)** What are you doing to my head?

Xanthula: Cleaning it, sweetie, of everything sticking to it… it's real dirty. **(Addressing Hedone)** Get me the medical antiseptic. **(Hedone goes, comes back immediately with a bottle, hands it over to Xanthula)**.

Socrates: But you are miscarrying the idea I was about to give birth to from my head.

Hedone: He's still hallucinating, milady… is there a man who gives birth!

Xanthula: **(Addressing Socrates)** So you're of the species that give birth, sweetie… your head gives birth… I wonder. Maybe you are like Zeus whose daughter Athena had been begotten out of his head.

Socrates: No… you don't understand and never will… my job as a philosopher resembles my mother who used to work as a midwife for pregnant women.

Xanthula: Don't remind me of her and her job, please. That's ancient history, we'd better forget it. Me, of the elite… my mother-in-law a midwife…

Socrates: **(Ignoring)** And I help myself and others to give birth to ideas; I am a midwife, begetting ideas.

Xanthula: **(Pouring the antiseptic over his head, giving it back empty to Hedone, addressing her)** Pour lots of water… we must rid him of all this dirt and contagious germs… the poor one thinking day and night, not sleeping at nights, wandering in the streets… and as you know, they're full of filth, and flies, and mosquitoes… and swamps. It all goes up to his head: no wonder he's bald…

Socrates: **(From under the water's dribble)** I'm almost suffocating... let me go… my eye… oh my eye…

Xanthula: **(After Hedone has poured all the water)** Hedone, bring me a lot of water… I need a whole river to clean up your master philosopher's head… as for his feet, it's hopeless to clean them… all our efforts will go down the drain… **(Hedone runs and comes back with another pot full of water; starts to pour it over Socrates' head)**

Xanthula: Enough… enough!

Hedone: Why, milady… we want to clean him up so well, that he may not go back to thinking again.

Xanthula: No, stupid… leave him as he is between sleep and awake… and bring me quickly the clothes and shoes… **(Hedone goes and is back with clothes and shoes; they immediately take to dressing up Socrates, after having done that, Socrates is somewhat alert)**.

Socrates: What's this... I feel as if in a dream… the whole world around me is strange… something new I haven't felt before **(Pointing at his wife)** …but I've seen that creature before! Where am I... such a strange dream! **(Looks around as Xanthula holds his arm, taking him out)**

Scene IV

The worst calamity makes one laugh

(Socrates in his new clothes and white shoes, all dressed up, Xanthula sitting close together on a high sofa at the right side of the hall, so as the audience may see them, as the different scenes of the play that they had come to watch take place on the stage)

Socrates: **(Muttering)** I'm about to suffocate… the robe is too tight… my feet inside the shoes are burning… I'm sweating… rivers of sweat are drowning me… I'm really drowning in my clothes and shoes! God… when will they start? When will they end?

Xanthula: **(With eyes wandering through around the hall here and there)** I thought I would be the most glamorous of ladies… I thought I would be the centre of attraction here… I paid a lot and uselessly. **(Sighing)** Alas! …of course the other women have real husbands who have real refined taste, able to buy clothes, make-up, perfumes, and gifts for their wives… of course each one of them can choose as she pleases by her own will all the clothes and make-up she needs… inspired by a great man who cares for her… But here am I, poor me… no one cares for me as though I live alone. **(Looks at Socrates finds him staring upward back to the state of meditation, she pinches him in the shoulder, kicking him with her foot, one of his soles flies away. Socrates becomes aware, he rises to pick up the shoe, crumbles down in his clothes, falls to the floor; on his face for a while).**

Socrates: Alas! Oh, my bones are crushed!

Xanthula: **(Suppressing her wrath as she tries to help him get up)** I'm done… I'm done! My shame… up man! Are you over-aged!?

Socrates: Haven't I told you that these clothes don't suit me? Let me leave this place to my real clothes, my real wide world, to my students **(Tries to leave)**.

Xanthula: Don't make a fool of us… sit down, sweetie… may Dionysus guide you… the show is about to start… **(They go back to their seats on the sofa, as the actors of the play within the play appear on the stage platform; the main actor is Aristophanes himself, a bit taller than Socrates, handsome, bright-faced; all the actors except**

Aristophanes holding in their hands masks for the characters whose roles they will play).

Aristophanes: (**Addressing the audience**) Before I wear the mask, you will recognize the role I'll play… I would like to advise you that I am both writer and director of this performance. I don't hold any animosity for any personality among us… for my only concern is the common welfare. I am only concerned with what can serve my country and the national Hellenic idea. And if I have criticized political leaders in previous plays relentlessly, without fear and hesitation, exposing political corruption of parties, and their bickering and administrative corruption everywhere, today in all honesty, being one of the intellectuals, I have decided to focus on self-criticism. That is to say that I, together with my colleague writers and men of letters and philosophers, may see ourselves in the mirror. Today, we will go deep into the cultural hypocrisy, and I will show you that artists and intellectuals coin new words, compatible with every age. They coin titles that they attribute to every new ruler. Here is an inspired ruler… another is hero of peace and war, and a third is the initiator of historical and geographical decisions.

Socrates: Geographical? It is unconceivable.

Aristophanes: Because he distributes vast lands on associates and relatives and family and kin, and so causes fundamental alterations on the topographic relief of the society.

Socrates: Ah… I understand… he exploits natural environment to cause upheavals in the social environment.

Aristophanes: And that's why they call him maker of geographical decisions. (**Adding**) And why do you wonder, Socrates, when the philosophers, who themselves are reformers, are often the instigators of corruption… for with their extremism they spread poison everywhere, they trade in people's emotions… misleading young… some intellectuals, gentlemen, seek the ruler's satisfaction and sympathy materially and morally at the expense of welfare…how often an artist sold himself to despots! All despots from Polycrates in Samos to Pisistratus in Athens… and Hieron in Syracuse, who recruited poets and artists to sing their virtues and glories, as for the philosophers whose thoughts are not understood by people, or who wishes to usurp the order of those things will have sold himself to the devil… and allow me now to start the show, free sons of Athens, builders of the pillar of civilization and defenders of the glory of democracy. You are the best audience who can relish fine comedy and react to it. (**To the actors**) I'll go in immediately to put on the role's clothes and mask. Let each one of you put on his mask as well (**Rushes inside; comes right back wearing rags like those of Socrates, on his face a mask precisely resembling that of Socrates; all actors wearing their masks. Aristophanes in Socrates' mask raises his head, stares in the sky, like the real Socrates does, with a bit of exaggerated comedy. Xanthula exchanging her gaze between the mask of Socrates and Socrates himself in wonder; discovers that the real Socrates too was gazing in the air. She kicks him with her foot. He becomes alert and realizes that Aristophanes will play his role on stage**).

Socrates: (**Rises**) Listen, Aristophanes, I object… you could have at least consulted me.

Aristophanes: If every writer consulted his hero he'd never write any literature, but only shallow historical recordings. And anyway you'll see through that show itself, that we have consulted your close friend Chaerephon. He is now cooperating fervently with us. (**Adding**) Don't you realize, Socrates, that you're in the theatre… you shouldn't start a dialogue with me… for whoever starts a dialogue with you is either an idiot or unfair to himself, unaware of the time… (**Puts the mask on his face**).

Socrates: This is…

Xanthula: (**She pulls him fiercely, makes him sit down**) Enough… have some respect for the theatre… don't make fools of us… let's start watching… it looks like a beautiful play indeed.

Socrates: Do you like this mask of which I've never seen anything uglier?

Xanthula: But it is exactly like you… the trouble with you is that you never look in the mirror… (**After a while**) You'd better shut up.

Socrates: Terrible catastrophe! Even you are against me…

Aristophanes: (**On stage addressing the audience, wearing the mask again**) Now everybody… please… silence… silence… please… we'll start the show immediately. (**Taps his foot on the floor three times, fixes the mask on his face; the play within the play starts**).

Socrates: (**In the play within the play, he ascends to the highest place on the stage platform, now and then he assumes a state of meditation staring in the air**) Who is this insect advancing towards us... of what era do you rush in the village ... and where do you come from, worm? (**The peasant looks around, doesn't answer**)

Socrates: Hey you... you worm, won't you answer, brother?

Peasant: Me, a worm... you dinosaur.

Socrates: If you know the size of the universe... oh, if only they drew it on a detailed map... you man, wouldn't occupy on it more than the place of a tiny insect, almost unseen with the naked eye, as it wanders in water-cress' field in particular?

Peasant: Water-cress field? Why? Do you know?

Socrates: (**Interrupting**) You're very stupid, you have neither field nor the mind... a peasant.

Peasant: Wrong... I've just come from a field of water-cress and I didn't see myself there... I mean I didn't see the worm... I...

Socrates: Idiot! You ask too many questions... all at once, and you don't give me a chance to answer them one by one...

Peasant: Alright... I'm listening.

Socrates: If you can stare in the sky... in a clear hour... and pierce the clouds with your sight... from a high place... as I am doing now, you could realize the size of the universe.

Peasant: And have you found out the size of the universe?

Socrates: Yes.

Peasant: That's why they called you the wisest of the wise... because you are in a moment of clarity... you have surpassed the clouds... and meditated in space. (**Adding**) But how many tons is the size of the universe?

Socrates: You, idiot... space is endless in size... I have learnt from my meditations in space, that the size of space cannot be estimated because it is unlimited and this infinitude is the closest estimation of the size of space.

Peasant: Great... so much for this matter... but I'm still at a loss at the relation between the water-cress field and the universe.

Socrates: You aren't to be blamed... for you don't follow the cultural symposia transmitted to the people by the eminent scholar, where he once said that water-cress possesses a mind that reaches down into the earth, giving it the nutrition… and this water-cress mind has its equivalent in everything in this wide universe.

Peasant: Yes, I heard people repeat these strange sayings, though I couldn't understand them. They also say that a clever lady grows water-cress under the bed and I still can't understand why!

Socrates: Wonderful!

Peasant: What?

Socrates: The fact that you're admitting that you don't understand means that you'll make a great philosopher.

Peasant: (**Angrily**) And who told you I want to be a philosopher? No, man, water-cress is better!

Socrates: At least you're ready to learn… the trouble with this nation is only in humbug… we find that someone who can't understand claims that he does… thus betraying himself and his nation… but you, you are blessed with modesty… I'll step down from my lofty position to teach you lessons (**He descends**).

Peasant: May Zeus, god of gods, bless and reward you…

Socrates: Idiot, don't even mention these gods in my presence again.

Peasant: And why, my honorable professor?

Socrates: These are outworn beliefs… there are now new trends in religion and conviction… so don't be backward... modernity… modernity.

Peasant: I don't understand!

Socrates: You're one wonderful idiot… how I like this phrase... coming out of your mouth as though it were a witty wise-saying… but you've got to widen your mouth like this when saying it (**Opens his mouth in a funny manner**)

Peasant: (**Opens his mouth imitating Socrates**) Like this… I don't understand!

Socrates: What a wonderful idiot you are! Alright… don't rush things… you'll understand… and now raise your head to the sky… and pierce the clouds with your eyes… huh. (**Peasant does as Socrates orders him**) Don't you see anything?

Peasant: Nothing.

Socrates: Focus your attention… and forget everything else around you…

Peasant: **(He does or tries to)**

Socrates: Huh… did you see anything?

Peasant: Nothing…

Socrates: You're not supposed to hear me, to forget your very existence… if you do that… surpass the clouds with your eyes, you'll find that the universe has its creative maker.

Peasant: And what's his name?

Socrates: He doesn't have a certain name for he has all names. He is the One hovering over all things and all beings. I can hear his voice calling me day and night… a voice comes to me with the light on a dark night… I see him in everything my hand touches… my eyes see… I feel him in the aroma of the flowers, in the scent of incense… it comes, floats with the breeze… driving before him ocean, and river waves… running through my blood inside my veins… I hear him with the beatings of the heart and the soul…

Peasant: And this state… when does it afflict you?

Socrates: It has no particular time… it comes rather suddenly.

Peasant: And this voice… what does it order you to do?

Socrates: Nothing… only belief and obedience… he says that if I obeyed his orders and avoided his prohibitions, I would attain all I wish from heaven in this world and in the next.

Peasant: But this is blasphemy, and atheism in the beliefs of the forefathers and the Olympian gods will not leave you.

Socrates: Olympian gods! Here you are… again going backwards… you're stupid… go back to your water-cress field under your bed, you'll fail in education… scram from my face (**Turns his face away**).

Peasant: **(Pleading)** My professor… my honorable professor… pretty patience… forgive me… I'm a peasant… and for the first time… I enter the city… these to me are new ideas… forgive me if I blunder or forget…

Socrates: Alright… I'll try another way with you, it's very simple (**Pauses a second)** Two men will come in now, imagine one of them is "Right" and the other is "Wrong" **(The two men enter, one a fat young man**

in fancy clothes with a sign on his chest saying: "Wrong" and his role played by Chaerephon. The other is a slim pale-faced old man dressed in semi-decent clothes, a sign on his chest where the word "Right" is written). Let these two men make a dialogue in front of you. You are to distinguish each of them and choose for yourself the path you like... come then let's sit aside and watch them (**He moves with the boy to the left side of the platform where they sit on the floor, as Socrates addresses the two men in the play within the play**). As for you, my dear students, as I taught you, you've got to do your very best in dialogue and convincing. We want the most useful meeting and the most violent discussion.

Wrong: I'll start talking... for I'm always ready and on the alert. (**Addresses Right**) As for you, you need a long time to pull yourself together... and even more time to understand what I say.

Right: And what have you got to mumble about? Or who will believe you, when you only emerge from wrong?

Wrong: (**Sarcastic**) And you don't speak of your own desire... You make me laugh and you make me cry too, because the worst calamity makes one laugh. Reality is clear before you and you deny it... or can't see it. It's one and the same... it seems that you've got weak eye-sight. (**After a while**) Believe me... I pity you because you live with the weak, the poor... As for my disciples, they are the masters in command... they're everywhere in every high status. They reside in paradise... you can see my friends in every gathering making speeches... their voices high, convincing... And you, where are your disciples?

Right: ...

Wrong: I'll answer for you... for reality to you is bitter and painful... your disciples are the rubbish of society... lurking at the bottom of the barrel, or they are in jails.

Right: Shut up! You roisterer... My friends are modest, satisfied with the little they've got, for they are content... and contentment is an endless treasure. They are fighting the corruption spreading throughout the country, and they may be even imprisoned and...

Wrong: (**Interrupting**) You mean to say that they are more like insects, walking through the streets in their shabby rags and barefoot... surrounded by flies... spreading epidemics, infecting environment with their ideas and rebelling on the settled situations. Whereas my disciples, they…

Right: **(Interrupting)** Thieves… bribed… abusing their power and prestige in illegal gains… they captured the state's possessions, built castles on them… dig rivers around them and build bridges or dig tunnels beneath them all that at the expense of the simple people, tax-paying.

Wrong: Stupid… my high-rank friends must have means of comfort so as to carry out their grave responsibilities efficiently.

Right: The state pays them big salaries.

Wrong: Not enough… you laggard, they've got many commitments and the modern newly invented equipments are highly expensive… **(After a while)** But let me ask about your disciples of the minor workers… is any one of them content with his salary, that doesn't even feed a cat? True, they've got big families… and still, they eat the best of meat, and chicken, and sweets… undoubtedly they also belong to those that you call "illegal". Don't they receive bribes? No one in this country lives only on his wages.

Right: But what a difference there is between one who is forced to blunder and one who does it because he is up to it, and enjoys it?

Wrong: This is a fallacy… for a theft is a theft… big or small… or do you call the thieves in the name of right among the just and honest people?

Right: **(Awkwardly)** Alright… alright do you mean that your disciples and mine are thieves because nothing distinguishes the one from the other, but the size of the position and the size of the theft.

Wrong: **(Screaming out of his role)** Oh, catastrophe!! Oh,…

Right: **(Out of his role)** What's wrong?

Wrong: You've led us to a dead end…

Right: How?

Wrong: For the first time, you and I agree so quickly!

Right: But don't say I'm stupid, because you don't realize that we live in an age where everything is all mixed up, so that there is no longer a difference between right and wrong… don't you agree to that?

Wrong: Yes, you're right… so let's exchange roles… replay our roles **(They shake hands and exchange labels)**.

Socrates: **(In the play within the play addressing the actors)** No… no… enough wasting time **(The actors leave, he addresses the peasant)**… Sorry, my dear… all my lessons and trainings have failed with these foolish students. **(He removes the mask, tosses it away and goes back to play the role of Aristophanes, and here the real Socrates rises approaching him)**

Socrates: My friend Aristophanes, allow me to tell you that your actors have reached a dead end in their dialogue for a very simple reason… it's so clear.

Aristophanes: And what is that?

Socrates: They're saying nonsense.

Aristophanes: But this is what actually happens.

Socrates: What do you mean?

Aristophanes: You for instance… you never give up or tire of talking day and night… so you spoil the minds of the young with whatever ideas you transmit… you're talkative, Socrates, and they call you the wisest of the wise… but you forget the most important wisdom the ancients left us: less said is a virtue.

Socrates: I don't transmit ideas into the minds of my students but I bring out whatever ideas are hidden within their minds… As to what the ancients said… I don't reject that completely but I have new ideas that look into the future.

Aristophanes: But your students, thanks to your teachings, refute everything that we found in our forefathers …they are breaking conventions and traditions in the name of advancement and modernity.

Socrates: This is the case… for you and your likes are conservative, even under-developed… you and your likes pull the people backwards resulting that other cities have surpassed us… like Thebes and Sparta.

Aristophanes: Now you confess that you prefer the Spartan totalitarian system to the Athenian democracy.

Socrates: I don't deny my admiration of the Spartan regime where law abides, and where people are equal in rights and duties, and where possessions are communal to all, no difference between young and old… where social justice reigns and class differences dissolve, and the educational Spartan system is quite austere.

Aristophanes: And I hate that regime that abolishes the personal freedom of individuals… interfering in people's affairs… big or small… I adore Athenian democracy... where each person has his own entity and his leading role in making things go… the people rule themselves and personal property is the foundation of the system.

Socrates: I agree with you… it was the Athenian democracy that led our armies to victory in Marathon and in the battle of Salamis, and it is under its rule that our state reached its golden age in the days of Pericles… But democracy today, which you fervently defend, is a corrupt democracy… fake… for on the inside it is rotten… all the parties are seeking the office… it is the ultimate end and lofty goal. As for the patriotic welfare, this is the only vehicle they use and it is the media propaganda that they exploit. We have no real opposition… Athenian democracy, Aristophanes, is over… it is difficult to save it.

Aristophanes: Socrates, I know that a dialogue with you never ends; the one involved in it with you is a goner, goner… Suffices for you to-day that you spoilt the theatrical show, and I'll lose the prize because of you, so please now leave us to do our work.

Socrates: You have no right to stop me from taking part in the performance that's ridiculing me in person.

Aristophanes: So we'll consult the audience, they represent the Athenian people… and the voice of the people is the voice of the gods.

Socrates: Alright… I don't trust this kind of popular referendum… but I've got to agree to your request.

Aristophanes: **(Addressing the public)** And now, freemen, so that our theatrical show may go on successfully, I suggest that Socrates be kicked out of this place. Do you agree?

A collective voice from the hall: We agree… we agree… we agree.

(The students gather around Socrates, start to pull him outside the place, and before the curtain drops, Chaerephon suddenly comes out from behind the curtain)

Chaerephon: Socrates… Socrates… Socrates… one minute please, Socrates.

Socrates: Hours if you will, Chaerephon… for a true friend always answers a friend's call.

Chaerephon: Please, Socrates, forgive me…

Socrates: **(Smiling)** Forgive you? What? You took part in this theatrical game?

Chaerephon: Surely I'll be defamed to have played a role in this comic play where I insulted you.

Socrates: Don't worry, for who is defended by virtue, sarcastic criticism can't do him any harm.

Chaerephon: But it's much more than that.

Socrates: **(Patting on his shoulder)** You're exaggerating the matter… it's important you don't blame yourself for everything, you've been lucky to take part in this play, which I don't think was intended to be insulting.

Chaerephon: Your words make my heart even burn more in remorse and all I can ask of you now is to forgive me if you realize the truth.

Socrates: What truth?

Chaerephon: The truth of what's going on around us.

Socrates: And do you think I'll reach the truth?

Chaerephon: If you don't, then humanity stands no chance of reaching any truth.

Socrates: Your opinion matches Apollo's oracle that you brought me from Delphi.

Chaerephon: **(Confused)** No. **(After awhile)** I wish I never went to Delphi. **(Adding)** I only want to assure you that it was my experience with you all these past years, and not the oracle, that has proved that you are indeed an unusual man.

Socrates: Strange… you, bearer of the oracle from Delphi… and only now your words agree with my response… not to accept it absolutely.

Chaerephon: Maybe… maybe… but there are different motives for each of us… only now do I understand why you refused to give in immediately to the oracle that called you the wisest of the wise… because you actually are the wisest of the wise… whether the oracle is true or false… **(He is talking to the audience)** People! Socrates is the wisest… People, there cannot be good in a nation that ridicules its wise men! People, defend Socrates like you would defend your own souls…

(The curtain)

ACT TWO

Scene I

Waiting for the Defeat

(The background of the stage is the depth of the sea; the inner platform represents the city walls, so that the stage platform is the area next to the city walls where Athenian women and children, men, young and old, are looking towards the sea in fear and anxiety).

Hedone: (**Handling her hair**) Milady, I do not understand why you are anxious and concerned over Socrates?

Xanthula: Strange... the whole country is in fear and danger... everyone is anxious and terrified, so can't I be as concerned and anxious as everybody else?

Hedone: (**Sweetly**) You are charming and beautiful... (**Runs her fingers through her hair and stares in her eyes**) It is not becoming to blemish your clear bright face with clouds of fear.

Xanthula: (**Moving back**) And how can one feel safe when everything around him indicates fear and plants anxiety in people hearts... Hedone, look at those people, their eyes staring into the void, their sights piercing the mountains, wandering the seas, in search for news... news of the war... all those people, be it man or woman, are burdened because he or she has a relative who went out to war and has never come back... may be a brother or a father... or a son or...

Hedone: (**Moving backward**) True... (**Gloomy**) Look at Helen over there at the end of the fence... with tears running down her face day and night... that they have dug a hot stream, pouring from the depth of her soul across the rocks to the sea where tears mix with the sea foam over slapping waves.

Xanthula: Can grief be to that extent?

Hedone: She has been on a hunger-strike for several weeks because her fiancé Paris is of the war heroes of whom no news has ever been received. He may be among those missing. I can understand the secret of her devastating grief; she will ultimately die if Paris does not return to her - that handsome Athenian young man who combines beauty and power in an unmatched manner.

Xanthula: **(Distracted)** Is he worth all that grief?

Hedone: She, who has such fiancé, can not live without him.

Xanthula: Strange... you speak sweet words and you live people's pain!!

Hedone: Look at Penelope there... that pregnant woman who embraces with her puffed stomach the temple column as though she would penetrate through it...she even kisses it from time to time... she has tried to commit suicide several times.

Xanthula: So she loves her husband that she would die of grief over him?

Hedone: She has completely lost her senses... maybe though she thinks that the column is her husband... I hate her.

Xanthula: Why?

Hedone: Her miserable absent husband is very rich and if he dies in war, the idiot will inherit his wealth. She and her children will enjoy all these riches... she will be the most valuable, I mean richest widow in Athens, and all suitors in love with her wealth will chase her... so why then would she grieve?

Xanthula: You are stupid... you are back to speaking nonsense again.

Hedone: I... I say but facts.

Xanthula: Facts?

Hedone: Yes... compare between the funeral of the poor and that of the rich.

Xanthula: How?

Hedone: In the funeral of the poor, the deceased's family and relatives cry bitterly... women slap their hearts and wail in the streets... they collect themselves in a funeral gathering encircling a clever mourner. The poor are not ashamed of grief, for they consider it natural.

Xanthula: True.

Hedone: As for the heirs of the rich, they walk behind the big huge coffin of the deceased in great prestige and reserve, they do not sob... maybe they do not even cry, justifying this as modernity, a religious and civilized behavior.

Xanthula: And do you have a different opinion?

Hedone: I am sure that their grief over the deceased, if any, is not honest, but rather mixed with a bit of joy over what they will inherit.

Xanthula: You are a devil... no one in his senses can believe you.

Hedone: Look at this circle (**Points to the left**). This woman there standing in the middle. She is Niobe carrying her infant with her ten daughters around her... she looks like a leader of the choral mourners... see how they slap their chests till they bleed... strong grief sweeps them, they keep swaying right and left... tearing their clothes... pricking locks of their hair... that they made a crowd of the people forget their grief and turn around her. They have decided to hold a cremation where they throw themselves alive into it to burn with the corpse of the head of this family, after having received news from the front confirming that he died while defending his site.

Xanthula: And what was the job of that man?

Hedone: A cobbler… a worker.

Xanthula: Alright... if poor and rich grief one way or another over the absence or death of their folk, then why wonder at my grief and...

Hedone: (**Interrupting**) Your attitude, my lady, puzzles me and your husband Socrates, I can not sort him among human beings.

Xanthula: You mean he does not deserve my concern and horror?

Hedone: But he hasn't died yet. The only news we received is that he has left his front position in the city of Amphipolis where the main Athenian force was stationed. He left the site and steeped himself in his meditations in the midst of his fans... he does that, there at the front! And of course, the enemies lay hold of the site and entered the city easily, and Socrates and his admirers are steeped in their meditations at the front... Be calm, milady! Your husband will go nowhere else. Surely he will return to Athens to make a dialogue with his students again in its alleys. He can not bear being away from Athens and his students... so do not worry he is coming. The life of the scamp lasts longest.

Xanthula: But he missed a valuable chance one that he doesn't come very often

Hedone: How?

Xanthula: I will explain... people here have become fed up with Socrates and…

Hedone: **(Interrupting)** And I know this pretty well?

Xanthula: Wait... **(Adding)** The rich hate Socrates because he has charmed their sons with his dialogues. They gathered around him leaving their rewarding jobs... I mean various investment projects like buying and selling of real estates, and the trade of import and export, a smuggling of currency. They left behind all these treasures and clung around Socrates... living the life of vagrants... forgetting the basic social manners of the aristocratic class.

Hedone: Indeed, they look horrible... neither becoming the rich nor the poor.

Xanthula: As for the poor who went to be tutored by Socrates, these despaired, for he teaches them philosophy and the art of dialogue... integrity, purity and obedience of laws... all of which neither fattens nor satisfies from hunger.

Hedone: But this is the first time in my life to hear the word "integrity". Do you mean strolling in the streets of Athens bare-footed like Socrates used to do?

Xanthula: No... no, stupid... "integrity" means "contentment".

Hedone: And is Socrates teaching the poor contentment?

Xanthula: Yes, for he is convinced that philosophy and art can never meet with wealth and prosperity.

Hedone: Only now can I understand the saying in our country they say about the poor and miserable: "the profession of literature caught them".

Xanthula: And now you can understand why the poor hate to find their children surrounding Socrates... because culture in our country is always associated with poverty and need, a pale face and psychic maladies.

Hedone: And with integrity... and contentment... and satisfaction with the least, terrible maladies.

Xanthula: And Socrates had to grasp the chance.

Hedone: How?

Xanthula: If he had done well, he would have rid himself of that public dissatisfaction and that ill reputation

Hedone: I think he will never succeed in that since he is hated by both rich and poor.

Xanthula: Maybe you're right. For what makes it worse is that it has been practically proved that he and his students are no good at war. Socrates may escape to exile without returning to Athens, as for...

Hedone: **(Interrupting)** I wish he could do.

Xanthula: **(Going on)** But if he does return home to the city, he will bring shame to me and my children. Have you heard the latest scandals?

Hedone: Scandals... more than that?

Xanthula: They say that after the defeat of our navy and the fall of tens of victims among our navy soldiers, the defeated leaders fled terrified without even pulling the corpses.

Hedone: Those cowards, they deserve the death penalty...

Xanthula: A military court convened, and Socrates was among its jury... the members and jury agreed on convicting these leaders on the grounds that they are traitors to the Hellenic blood. And that they deserve the death penalty.

Hedone: That is a just verdict.

Xanthula: No one objected but Socrates, for he confronted this consensus claiming that he generally rejects the death sentence, saying that a live dog is better than a dead lion, as he defended the lives of those cowardly leaders.

Hedone: And such strange situations are not new to your husband.

Xanthula: **(To herself)** How will I face my aristocratic family with their glorious military feats? They will insult me... I married Socrates against their strong opposition.

Hedone: Do you want my advice?

Xanthula: Only if it is a wise one.

Hedone: Ask for a divorce.

Xanthula: But the new personal statute law is so cruel on the one who causes divorce... as for the woman, who seeks break-up, is stripped from everything but her clothes.

Hedone: Alright... let him seek a divorce.

Xanthula: How?

Hedone: You ask how? Aren't you a woman?

Xanthula: If you mean to make his life miserable... I am doing it all the time... and he still goes out of the house smiling. Besides, he spends most of his time outside domestic wedlock: he is married to philosophy, has divorced comfort and preferred to be a bohemian wandering in the streets of Athens. (**She hears separate shouts; everybody is directing their eyes towards the sea watching the approaching ships**).

A woman voice 1: Here are the ships, there in the horizon.

A woman voice 2: I wish you were among the comers, dear husband!

A woman voice 3: What is important is to be back with victory.

A voice of an old man: The news of victory comes on the wings of wind… and if they have really won, we'd have learned of their victory before their return.

A woman voice 1: Here are the ships approaching… they're about to touch the shore… but where are the victory flags?

A woman voice 3: If the victory flags haven't turned up till now, this means that they… they… are defeated.

All voices: Defeated… Oh? Athens is defeated… the citadel of democracy has fallen… the fortress of freedom... what devastation! (**Everybody starts wailing bitterly; they scream, clap their chests; dance to funeral dances while singing**).

Athens… Athens

Nation of strong prosperity

Fallen into the sea

Drowned… drowned

They have beaten you… beaten you

Who?

The enemies… the enemies
No
The dear children
Yes
Those… are those
They quarreled… they fought
They lagged behind… they were slackened
Forsook right and sought wrong
Cheated in selling
Deceived one another
So their ships were lost at sea
The flags of victory fell off their hands
Will live for years in humiliating captivity
They'll drink the cup of defeat and subjugation
Athens… Athens
You ancient city
Defeat came from within
So may the will strengthen
There is no hope for redemption
Till we conquer self
Overcome corruption
Let's crush our failings
Let's crush our failings
Let's crush our failings

(Socrates enters with some of his students, fatigue of travel on their faces. Socrates goes to his wife and Hedone)

Socrates: My dear wife… good evening, Xanthula… you left the children at home to join these funeral dances?

Xanthula: Yes… me of all women I've earned it… for each one of them weeps over something, but I, I weep over things… and things. This one may be weeping over the loss of her son or injury of a brother, or the loss of the husband but I…

Socrates: **(Interrupting)** Crying over the fall of a democracy or…

Xanthula: **(Interrupting)** And what have I got to do with democracy, let it go to hell… I'm crying over the shame that befell me… **(To herself, crying)** Your bad luck, Xanthula.

Socrates: You mean that the defeat of Athens' democracy has brought you shame… then you are great! **(He is about to embrace her)**.

Xanthula: **(Interrupting and pulling away)** I told you I don't care for democracy and its fall.

Socrates: What shame then?

Xanthula: Yours.

Socrates: Strange… me a shame! **(Looks at himself up and down, turning around)**.

Xanthula: No…. no… I don't care for your ragged clothes now.

Socrates: So how do I bring shame upon you then?

Xanthula: You're still asking me? You know that my father was the best of cavalry and my great grandfather was a courageous invader who conquered capitals, crushed walls and annexed countries.

Socrates: **(To himself)** She still lives imprisoned in her outworn past!

Xanthula: And you come along leaving your front position to the enemy, to pierce into the Athenian front forces and conquer them, and take Amphipolis… did you forget that you are my husband?

Socrates: How can I forget?

Xanthula: You brought shame upon my family… and my children by you.

Hedone: (Still engaged in funeral dancing) Oh, catastrophe! How can I hide my face with this shame?

Socrates: You too, Hedone are struck by my behavior at war.

Xanthula: It's a grand treason, Socrates, to the family honor that you became related by marriage to it since a long time, and whose honor you should have defended.

Socrates: Won't you listen to the explanation of my situation?

Xanthula: It's all too clear… needs no explanation.

Socrates: The simplest of matters always needs explanation more than any other, for these simple matters most of the time can deceive people with its simplicity, and if you discuss them carefully, you may discover that they're not that simple.

Xanthula: You're complicating matters. I don't understand what you're saying.

Socrates: Then… quite simply you can be proud of your husband.

Xanthula: The deserter… the careless… the traitor?

Socrates: That's precisely what needs an explanation.

Xanthula: How?

Socrates: I'll answer… what is democracy?

Xanthula: You keep asking… never answering.

Socrates: And sometimes a question is its answer.

Xanthula: I don't understand.

One of Socrates' students: Shall I answer, Professor?

Socrates: Alright… you've grown up, Plato and you can answer.

Plato: Democracy is prosperity for all… equality… freedom… safety and peace, sovereignty of the law.

Socrates: Good…

Xanthula: And Athenian democracy was not so?

Socrates: It was so… in the days of Pericles the Great. (**After a pause**) This war in which Athens was defeated where did it take place? At the far north, at the Chalkidike Gulf… Athens and Sparta - the former in the middle of the Greek mainland, and the latter - in the south, and war between them going on in the north… this quick geographical glimpse at things reveal that it is not a war for peace or freedom… it is one of despotism… of expansion… each of the neighboring states aspires to control the Hellenic world… and he, who seeks to impose his will with force, is not democratic. And from the moment when Athens got involved in this war, it was no longer a democratic state… since then, and not just now, it's pathetic.

Xanthula: Whatever the case… you should have upheld your country's cause.

Socrates: The issue of patriotism is beside the point… for war between two neighboring cities is considered to be a civil war, neither victorious nor defeated for everybody is crushed. And you may ask me why then did I go to war?

Xanthula: Yes… why?

Socrates: In accordance to blind obedience to the state and its laws… But do you know what made me stop fighting?

Xanthula: No… what?

Socrates: News broke out that the opponents,… **(Adding)** I mean the Spartans, have received a big deal of weapons from the Persians… so, after disarming ourselves, me and my students, we sat down to discuss the matter. Some of them were filled of zeal to fight by this very deal as it meant that Sparta was allying with the enemies of the Hellenic nation, in order to conquer its brothers… and all for the sake of leadership.

Xanthula: They're right.

Socrates: But I asked my students this question: Where do our arms come from?

Xanthula: And what was the answer?

Socrates: From Carthage in the far west.

Xanthula: I still don't understand at all.

Socrates: I explained to my students that neither the Persians in the east nor the people of Carthage in the west care for democracy to flourish in the lands of the Hellenes, because each of the two states follows a despotic system… so I decided together with my students not to continue in combat… and thus we left the site.

Xanthula: So the Spartans captured the site.

Socrates: And why does this bother you? Greeks captured Greek land. **(After a pause)** Anyway, we went into an extended dialogue with the Spartans and…

Xanthula: **(Interrupting)** You went to fight, and not to make a dialogue.

Socrates: **(Adding)** And when we tried to convince them to stop fighting… and that we are their brothers… fellows… But their zeal for war and their stubbornness were not less violent and fierce than that of the Athenians… so we left them alone.

Xanthula: That's not important… tell me now why didn't they capture you and your students? **(Adding)** That's the point.

Socrates: It seems that they were afraid of our ideas, so they set us free to get rid of us. **(Andocides enters)**

Andocides: Socrates… the enemies are tightening the siege around you, while you are still here steeped in argument.

Socrates: I don't care what others do, and what plots they devise, all this can't affect me in the least. Nothing can harm me, but what my own hands commit… for he who is strong, no one can harm.

Andocides: But you'll stand trial soon.

Socrates: Court?

Andocides: Yes, for Antinous has presented a legal petition against you, and two men signed with him accusing you of atheism, and of corrupting youth, and resisting the democratic system… It's a tight circle that will tie around your neck, so what are you doing about it?

Socrates: Nothing… because ill cunning upturns only on its owners.

Andocides: At least prepare an eloquent speech in your defence.

Socrates: Why?

Andicides: To escape penalty.

Socrates: If I really deserve punishment, let it be… and let the law take its course. Besides, I'm busy these days in a dialogue with my students about an important issue that one of them raised.

Andocides: But the matter concerns your very life and you must be saved.

Socrates: Me, saved?

Andocides: It seems you don't appreciate the gravity of the situation... **(After a pause)** In any case, I'm not a philosopher, I'm a lawyer, and my job is to write speeches in defence at courts... so allow me to make you a defence speech.

Socrates: Death to me is better than to resort to this manner... for your job is to beat around the bush in legal texts and appealing procedures... you maneuver and evade the law, and this is not in accordance with my principles.

Andocides: So you'll not attend the trial?

Socrates: This is a worse crime... I will attend the trial as I should, for the law requires my presence.

Xanthula: **(Interfering)** So, you must defend yourself, Socrates, if not for yourself, so for your children.

Socrates: I'm confident of my innocence and I don't care if I'm convicted by whose justice I don't trust... **(He points at his wife)** And now let's go back to our children, I miss them.

Xanthula: Alright... let us go... **(Lags that she may whisper in Andocides' ear)** Prepare yourself to articulate a defence speech, I'll pay your fees myself.

Scene II

Victory of the Defeated

(Areopagus court; at the rear is the Acropolis rock, the court being a platform higher than the stage, on top of which are two rows of wooden or brick seats, each six seats; sitting on them are the twelve members of the jury including the head, who is Democratia, sitting in the front right. At the far left of the stage is a small platform on which Socrates stands accused; at the far right is a similar platform on which Andocides stands, as being the representative of the petitioners. The jury members are wearing Greek outfit, Democratia holds a scepter of the justice - a cane crowned by the head of goddess Athena; Xanthula and Hedone sit among the audience in the hall).

Democratia: **(She knocks three times with her cane)** In the name of goddess Athena... In the name of Athenian democracy, we inaugurate this session. Hence, citizens, sons of Athens, the case today are an important case for the suspect is a personality known to you all. A friendship has been between us for a long time... the accusations facing our friend Socrates are serious. Allow me to read you the law suit, presented to the court. Allow me formally **(Sharp clapping)**. "In the name of the sovereignty of the law, and in the name of Themis goddess of justice, and Athena goddess of wisdom, and in the name of Athenian democracy, we who sign below present this petition of accusation to the honorable court versus Socrates, son of Sophilos. The one in mention has taken odd actions and shameful and suspicious acts, besides spreading various strange sayings. These sayings and these actions tend to ruin Athenian democracy and break down social structure, and turn all things upside down. Socrates for example, claims to walk in the air, mixes with creatures in space, studies what is beneath the earth and above the clouds, can turn wrong into something close to sheer right. Most dangerous of all is that Socrates believes in one god thus denouncing all Olympian gods and our fore-fathers' religions. He claims that he is the messenger from merciful Providence to human beings, and that the God he believes in converses with him now and then, in voices only he can hear. Socrates has corrupted youth, for he has implanted in their minds these heresies and convictions. And teaching in childhood is like inscription on stone. Every catastrophe that has befallen our city is because of Socrates' devastating principles. According to the fore-mentioned, we demand from the honorable court to summon Socrates to a public trial.

Signatures:

Additional Note: We offer the present proxy to Andocides to stand on our behalf before the honorable court during the trial. **(Noise in the hall expressing astonishment)**

Xanthula: Honorable president, Andocides took money from us… lots of money to defend my husband Socrates. He represents Socrates, not his adversaries.

Democratia: **(Knocking her cane)** I am committed to the formal delegation attached to the petition.

Xanthula: And what about my money that I paid Andocides?

Democratia: This is not the business of the court… and you may send a petition against him.

Xanthula: But my husband will stand before you defenceless.

Democratia: To prove the impartiality of the court, we'll give Socrates a last chance so that he can now ask one of the lawyers to represent him in his defence. **(Light focuses on Socrates).**

Socrates: No, president of court, your generous offer is refused. If Socrates accepts someone to defend him, then he is not Socrates.

Xanthula: For the sake of your children, Socrates … **(She weeps)** for the sake of the family honor. **(Socrates turns away angrily, as Lysias the famous lawyer advances from the hall)**

Lysias: Our Professor Socrates, there is no one in Athens who does not know me… for I have, many a time, saved poor suspects, saved them from prison or death, saved them from their adversaries' strong claws, saved them from the labyrinths and maneuvers of spiral laws and bureaucratic regulations, so allow me, great Socrates, to gain this honor by defending you in this case…huh… allow me to start my defence…your…

Socrates: **(Interrupting)** And what is your ultimate goal in your defence?

Lysias: Your acquittal of course.

Socrates: And this is not my goal.

Lysias: Then what is your goal?

Socrates: To reach the truth.

Xanthula: **(Interfering)** Socrates… Socrates, you're in court, my dear, not at school… no need for philosophy here.

Socrates: **(Continuing)** We should seek the truth everywhere, at all times.

Democratia: And now, Socrates, what is your final decision… are you authorizing someone to defend you or not?

Xanthula: **(Quickly)** Yes, we'll authorize Lysias.

Lysias: **(Immediately)** Yes, I represent him.

Socrates: **(Firm and calm)** …no…no…no one represents Socrates in his defence. **(Xanthula goes to Lysias grabbing his clothes)**

Xanthula: Give me my money then?

Lysias: I owe you no money, my lady. I came to court, I tried to do my duty, but your husband stopped me, is it my fault?

Democratia: **(Knocks strongly with her cane)** Everyone be seated in his place, and let's have complete silence. The matter has been decided and Socrates will defend himself… Let us then start the trial… Of course, we will listen first to the speech of the representative of the prosecution please. **(Light focuses on Andocides standing alert; noise of disapproval in the hall; Democratia knocks her cane)**

Andocides: Memb… **(Interrupted by the noise of disapproval; Democratia knocking her cane; the noise stops)** Members of the jury, your Excellency, the supreme chief of the court, **(Turns to the hall)** ladies and gentlemen, in the name of justice I greet you. **(Disapproving laughter in the hall)** I swear by all Olympian gods that I shall abide by the truth and honesty and not by personal interest or career… for my only concern is to face this complicated case in the common interest and security of the country, and the individuals, and their welfare and prosperity. We must all seek to protect their basic principals of democracy under the protection of our wise government, led by the inspired maker of historical decisions, Democratia. **(Sharp clapping from the hall, mainly from women)**

Democratia: **(Knocks with her cane addressing Andocides in humble tone)** Please, start directly, sir… There is no need to prolong the introduction **(Turns to the hall knocking her cane)** Silence please… let justice take its course. **(Women in the hall shouting: "Long live**

the inspired chief... with blood... with souls, we offer up Democratia". Democratia knocks violently).

Andocides: My defendant, your Excellency the president…

Democratia: **(Interrupting)** I am here head of the court, sir, be accurate, and Athenian jurisdiction has its traditions and is known for its fairness.

Andocides: It is to the country's good fortune that you combine in your wise hands, the legislative and the legal authorities, together with the political authority, we wish you'd represent the rest of the authorities, for this is a gods' blessing to the Athenians.

Democratia: Resume your defence.

Andocides: The petitioners, members of the jury, are of the most noble families in Athens, they are of its finest sons… those who have been as faithful, as dedicated, in the service of the patriotic cause… they diligently served democracy, remember the day they paid the donation to build the fleet with thousands of talents... Do you remember one of them who gave up some parts of his commercial fleet to be transformed into naval ships? And the one who gave up vast areas of grapes for the sake of our army and the military efforts, how could we forget? True, they are wealthy, but they are noble… patriotic capitalists. Don't believe the lies spread about them, for biased opportunists said that they became rich because of the wars… this is a fallacy, that can conceal behind it nothing less than envy and spite. Yes envy, gentlemen, is the vice of our society—it's not the fault of these honest citizens. If it turned up that the ships they had offered were with holes? Or that the food they offered the armed forces was rotten? Can we blame them? Are we to judge them that these ships sank at sea before any combat with the enemy? Or should we judge those responsible for these ships, for failing to fix them before the battle? And those who ate the rotten food and were poisoned, why didn't they smell it before eating it? Gentlemen, no stronger proof there is of the faithfulness of the petitioners to the homeland and to democracy than this law suit against Socrates **(Noise in the hall).**

Democratia: **(Knocks with the cane)**

Andocides: **(Continuing)** I, personally, am one of Socrates' students and fans, I love him very much. **(Laughter in the hall)** For he has a beautiful personality… see his countenance… how beautiful **(Noise in the hall).**

Democratia: **(Knocks with the cane)**.

Andocides: Yes, I loved him, but he was soon exposed. I thought he was the faithful honest man… I took him for an honorable professor, I considered him savior of the country, liberator of minds from corruption… I was enchanted by his words, but I soon became aware, and returned to my senses.

Democratia: Be precise… explain exactly what you want to say.

Andocides: I ask, your Excellency, as superior chief of this court… where is your son Democratos? **(A pause)** He's gone to wander in the streets of Athens aimless… isn't that so? A young man of thirty has learnt nothing yet, never did a useful craft… never obtained useful knowledge… left industry and commerce, and investment, and the exchange bureaus only to become a student of Socrates… and our son Democratos is lost! Although he does speak lofty and elegant sounding words and is good at maneuvering in dialogue… but he ends up as nothing but a vagrant and rascal.

Democratia: **(Nervously hitting the floor with her cane and feet)**

Andocides: **(Adding)** And what is your son, virtuous lady… that dirty hypocrite, if not one of the preposterous examples of the loss of this generation, brought up and fed on Socrates' words… it is a generation worthy of annihilation. **(Noise, whisperings of rejections in the hall)**

Democratia: **(Knocking the floor nervously)** You have trespassed your limits… remember your principle mission.

Andocides: I beg your pardon, my lady for I am fed up. For corruption in the young people has reached its extreme dimensions limits… youth nowadays, most virtuous lady, are far from polite; in the past, any young man would never dare to harass any girl in the street. People used to beat violently who would attempt it… and I, personally, had an unforgettable experience. I was a strong sturdy muscular young man, and one day a charming girl in a popular Greek robe passed before me like a turf branch… gliding, her hips swaying and… **(Noise)**

Democratia: **(Knocking her cane)**

Andocides: To make a long story short… I tried to approach her, to touch any part of her body… she took off her left shoe and took to beating me. To tell you the truth the beatings of her sandals were soft and acceptable… but soon I found hands from all directions beating me violently and intolerably… all the neighbors' men were surrounding me, left me no less than out cold… after having regained my consciousness, I decided not to harass any girl whether wrapped in a traditional robe, or even almost naked as Spartan girls are fond to be these days. For I was raised up according to the morals of the past… But today young men harass not only girls, but married women, even walking in the arms of their husbands… to the extent, that girls and women are kidnapped from vehicles and streets…anyone walking in the public meeting place could read everyday ostraca of strange advertisements like…"a beautiful girl went out, never returned"… "a married lady disappears in mysterious circumstances… whoever finds her, contact house no 67".

Democratia: And do you find that Socrates is behind all these crimes? I don't suppose he likes women?

Andocides: I really don't think he likes women… and here is the great problem. Socrates is the cause of corruption.

Democratia: How?

Andocides: It is he who has led a strong campaign of skepticism against our gods, the Olympus gods, whom we inherited from our ancestors. It is he who has led youth to aspire to change everything and to destroy everything… in the name of renovation and modernity. They no longer have a religious drive or traditions; have no respect for laws or conventions. They commit every violation and possess the power to justify it.

Democratia: Have you any other accusations?

Andocides: **(Scratching his head)** Socrates is leading an eccentric way of life… and I wonder how young people forsake life's pleasures and temptations, only to surround this pale-faced… bare-feet.

Democratia: Do you have any more to say?

Andocides: No…

Democratia: Then you'll remain silent, don't interrupt Socrates when he starts to defend himself… he spoke no word during your speech. **(Turns to Socrates to speak)** Now it's your turn, Socrates… start your defence.

Socrates: Alright… thank you… honorable lady… and thanks to all members of the honorable court. I confess from the beginning that I am not eloquent in making speeches, I even can't find the art of articulation… thus I'm no rhetorician, although I envy rhetoricians for their rhetoric and eloquence, and I'll address you in simple language - the ordinary language that I speak in my daily life. I am aware that I am in a very awkward situation and that my case is quite serious… for those, who point at me accusing me openly and secretly, are more than I can count or even know of… for even since Aristophanes ridiculed me in one of his comedies, people were perplexed; they said that I am meditating on the supernatural… and that I walk on air in search of new gods. All this I have not the honor to think of, let alone refute? Allow me my great honorable lady, to call on my adversary, not to answer to the accusation, but to uncover the truth…I shall pose before you some questions and…

Democratia: **(Interrupting)** But you are here to answer not to ask questions, Socrates.

Andocides: And I object strongly for the defence is not pursuing the legal procedure mentioned in Article 5/6 with a dash… I will not answer any question… save me, my lady, he wants to examine me!

Socrates: Fear not Andocides, for I am the accused here, not you… besides, my questions will be quite simple—so answer what you know, and avoid answering each time you find yourself unable to say the truth.

Andocides: Alright…

Socrates: My first question is very simple: **(Firmly)** are you fully convinced that the accusations held against me are true?

Andocides: This is a bullet not a question? You want to destroy me completely.

Socrates: You refuse to answer?

Andocides: No I will.

Socrates: Honestly?

Andocides: In all honesty I say that I'm fully convinced of all these accusations.

Socrates: And your proofs?

Andocides: This corruption that has spread throughout the city… people love each other no more… each person seeks to grasp any profits in the horizon, if even over the ruins of others… grabbing is the prevalent system… in everything even in the road… every human being wants to ride the road all to himself, be it a man or a woman, people in our country crowd over everything, they even fight among themselves over air, they've left not one centimeter of desert.

Socrates: Yes, I agree with you … that is true. Corruption is spread throughout the city, has infiltrated the souls of people… I admit my responsibility for that corruption… but as one of the educated only…

Andocides: You started with a clear and right beginning, and ended up in mystery… for half your words are unintelligible.

Socrates: It is the duty of the intellectuals in this country to undertake the lead and pioneering, each of them has to be a good example for others… and maybe I haven't done my duty as I should, in this respect.

Andocides: So you confess to the accusation of negligence?

Socrates: Perhaps…but…tell me… weren't it you yourself a student at my school?

Andocides: (**Comes closer to Socrates and whispers in his ear**) Yes, my professor… and frankly those were sweet days when I had dear fellows, innocent friends… your lessons were enjoyable. (**Raises his voice slowly**) but… I mean I quit your school a long time ago.

Socrates: How? Why?

Andocides: My father took me from your school to another, he then told men that Socrates' school is ill-famed, and to convince me he reminded me that Socrates' students in "***The Clouds***" had burnt that school.

Socrates: And where did you resume your learning?

Andocides: Under Protagoras the Sophist.

Socrates: He is a virtuous man… you are lucky to have had that professor.

Andocides: He felt the same for you, even was like you in some ways…but he focused his efforts on teaching speeches.

Socrates: And is this how you have become an eloquent speaker?

Andocides: I assure you that the money my father paid him was worth it… for I have greatly acquired the professional oratory, and the legal profession. (**Approaching Socrates gently**) As for you, my professor, (**Whispering**) don't be angry with me (**Raising his voice**) for you are still poor in rags… bare-footed… professor, you should have given private lessons… your colleagues now are among the wealthiest of the wealthy. (**Whispers in Socrates' ear**) I care for your own good… I'm only advising you. (**Adding**) But anyway it's too late now. (**Raising his voice**) But I notice that you've led me on, away from our present situation… the trial.

Socrates: Not at all… we're not far… we're getting to the core of the case… and this is clear in your words.

Andocides: My words… in the core of the case?

Socrates: It seems that like me you find that reforming the nation starts with the educational system because the student who clowns or cheats for instance, is the future chaotic soldier, who deserts the battlefield from the very first moment. The same student could be a physician in the future, but of the type that steals the patients' money and life at the same time.

Andocides: Quite true.

Socrates: And what do you think of a lawyer who collects huge amounts of money from both parties of the legal dispute?

Andocides: (**Hesitant**) A corrupt thief, robbing peoples' money without a scrap of conscience or modesty.

Socrates: The important thing is that it is the outcome of a corrupt educational system, isn't it?

Andocides: Surely.

Socrates: Do you expect that lawyer to speak the truth?

Andocides: Surely not… but I find that we have really got out of the subject.

Democratia: Alright… alright… on my part, I find that we're quite close to the end.

Andocides: I too have this feeling and I ask you a definite question… will you answer clearly and frankly?

Socrates: Of course.

Andocides: How do you justify the environmental pollution in our city? Where does this black cloud come from when our sun has been shining since antiquity? And where does all this dirt that has become the prevailing feature of our city streets, inviting summer maladies and winter epidemics, come from? **(Adding)** Luckily for us, our country knows only these two seasons in the year…

Socrates: These very questions diagnose the state of our city…for the underground swamps have become an inseparable part of the features of the Athenian street. These swamps flow and cover vast areas in each district; they don't dry them although they have an odor that hurts noses. I don't know… have people lost their sense of smell?

Andocides: **(Forgets about himself and approaches Socrates)** Have you heard the latest joke?

Socrates: No…

Andocides: **(Approaches Socrates, Democratia approaches to listen to the joke)** One morning one of the citizens left his house… to find one of these flowing underground swamps… couldn't cross to the other side… he just stood there, not knowing what to do…but he soon saw another person at the far end of the road, so he wondered and cried loudly: hey…hey…how did you cross to the other side? The answer came from far…no…no…it's nothing, I was born here…

Socrates: …

Andocides: Won't you laugh over this joke?

Socrates: Rather I wonder at a city that drowns in filthy underground water and never lose their sense of humor.

Democratia: **(Knocks with her cane)** Once more you're out of the subject.

Andocides: We'll be back to the core of the matter, and I'll ask Socrates… why are people inclined to filth?

Socrates: I don't know… it's a matter that calls for meditation.

Andocides: In the past, there was a principle: purity is essential in our faith, and people would clean themselves before entering temples of gods… but now everything has changed.

Socrates: And why?

Andocides: Because people no longer go into temples… they have lost faith… and no purity.

Socrates: What do you mean exactly?

Andocides: What I mean is as clear as daylight, your teachings have led the people to lose faith in the gods…there is no purity of body and soul for the faithless.

Socrates: A sound principle indeed…I mean it may be so…but you're applying it to me…and that's a mistake.

Andocides: You don't practice what you preach…in the name of the gods I implore you, didn't you look once in the mirror?

Socrates: I don't like mirrors.

Andocides: I wish you could… so that you'd know that your very looks are a bad example for your students…can't the intellect and meditation be compatible with cleanliness?

Socrates: You're interested in physical appearance neglecting looking deeper into matters and their essence.

Andocides: And how can we separate appearance from the essence of matters? Doesn't each pot reflect what's within it? (**Sharply**) Socrates…Socrates…I say it clearly…the fact that you stand here in court…in your shabby rags and bare-feet is considered an underestimation to the honorable court and solid proof that you have actually corrupted our youth …and I demand that the honorable court issues the death sentence as punishment for all the crimes that you have committed…or otherwise to be exiled from Athens for life.

Democratia: Have you got anything to add, in your defence Socrates?

Socrates: I have said enough.

Democratia: And you Andocides?

Andocides: Nothing.

Democratia: (**Coming closer to Andocides and whispers in his ear**) But you forgot so much.

Andocides: So much…like what?

Democratia: Opium and olive and…

Andocides: **(Adding, addressing Socrates)** Really, Socrates…I forgot to dialogue with you in two important matters.

Socrates: We've plenty of time and I welcome your dialogue.

Andocides: Aren't you one of the education-makers in our country?

Socrates: So they say.

Andocides: But I can almost doubt that you're a real intellectual.

Socrates: I wish you'd be clear…perhaps help me understand the reality of myself.

Andocides: I noticed that you don't smoke or chew green opium leaves.

Socrates: And what are these leaves?

Andocides: Green drugs that the ancients used in medicine but these days the so-called intellectuals in our country use great amounts of it in chewing and smoking.

Socrates: How?

Andocides: They make out of these grasses rolls, that they fill with more dried leaves, crushed or mashed…then they light fire in one of its tips and draw the drug from the other end, by mouth…they enjoy it greatly.

Socrates: Wonder! They enjoy the smoke which pollutes the environment?

Andocides: They say…that it is this smoky atmosphere that helps them to receive inspiration…so they create the sweetest of verses…the smoke of that grass takes them to soar in the horizons of imagination and inspiration…by which they reach the very gods on top of Olympus and Parnassus.

Socrates: Then most of our intellectual folks are drug addicts.

Andocides: Yes drug addicts.

Socrates: But culture represents the mind of a nation… so that if it is absent by addiction, the mind is lost.

Andocides: And you are the one responsible for all that.

Socrates: How is that when I never ever even tasted that smoke?

Andocides: You are the generation teacher... and you bear the responsibility of corrupting it.

Socrates: I assure you, and the honorable lady, Democratia, and the distinguished jury, that I have never called for an art that is not based on a conscious mind. I am against art for art's sake...neither do I believe in sheer inspiration in art...as I have announced frankly in my dialogue with the epic singer Ion... old and young in Athens know that.

Andocides: But your action contradicts your claims, remember the day you were walking outside the walls' of the city by the river bank...watching the setting sun...your face in the sky with distracted eyes...your bare feet steeped into thorns and mud...unaware of everything around you, till you fell into the river still watching the setting sun...you almost drowned and you even forgot that you could swim...remember that day?

Socrates: Yes, I remember.

Andocides: Since that time you became one of the drug addicts, I mean the intellectuals and the artists.

Socrates: But the habit of forgetting or steeping in contemplation is one thing, but affecting this or even seeking it is another.

Andocides: The important thing is that the intellectuals took you as their model...they tried hard to lose the self...to lose consciousness and awareness of the truth at any cost, claiming that in this way they are more fit, and ready to create.

Socrates: This is a serious matter...

Andocides: More serious still, is that these grasses have risen in price...and are in constant rise...for two reasons: one, is the great demand for it, second is that the state has interfered, banned its planting and importing...and hence its trafficking.

Socrates: It did well.

Andocides: But it had completely averse results...gangs were formed to embezzle these grasses into the country...and sell it at unimaginable prices...

Socrates: And why don't they arrest the smugglers?

Andocides: Because some of them are from the authorities.

Socrates: So they leave people like that?

Andocides: Merchants of these grasses are wealthy people… and they control the country's economy…even its policy…as for the addicts, these pay from their folks' very bread and their dependants' for the sake of their mood.

Socrates: This is a case of complete devastation…a hopeless case.

Andocides: And you're responsible.

Socrates: I don't care to refute this accusation, for my heart breaks over this loss.

Democratia: Enough discussion over this matter, Andocides… let's move to other accusations.

Andocides: I have no other accusation.

Democratia: **(Coming closer to Andocides whispers in his ear)** Did you forget?... the rats?

Andocides: **(Adding addressing Socrates)** Excuse me… excuse me, Socrates… I have one last question.

Socrates: Ask what you will… we're in no hurry.

Andocides: You know that our country is one of the most fertile in the world… in the past it used to be a warehouse for crops and food' for ancient empires… we used to export the surplus of our agricultural products to the whole world…wheat, beans, lentil, grapes, olives, and…

Socrates: Yes…yes…these are well known facts…even boys at school know it, for they always say that our country is an agricultural country.

Andocides: And now it's the other way round, we are now importing everything, including beans and lentil… everyday you can see queues of the hungry increasing in length before food stores, even bread is in queues…for long hours.

Socrates: What really puzzles me generally, is a person's rush over food, and on the imported food in particular, although most of it is rotten.

Andocides: Have you asked yourself of the secret behind this deterioration?

Socrates: To tell you the truth…I didn't care much for that…what interests me is the food of the mind…not in satisfying bellies…

Andocides: And this is the catastrophe, the intellectuals here are aloof from reality…you for instance have stuffed the minds of the youth with strange sayings and odd teachings…that corrupted them and here we are now.

Socrates: How? Enlighten me.

Andocides: You told people you preferred a life of meditation to one of manual labor.

Socrates: Yes… I love meditating and I hate handicrafts.

Andocides: It's become a shame to the minds of youth to work in these crafts, they despise them…so they left their work either to surround you…or to stroll in the streets in meditation, or else to emigrate outside the country.

Socrates: And what do they do there?

Andocides: They are exposed to the worst of treatment… he who leaves his own home, loses respect.

Socrates: But exactly what do they do?

Andocides: The problem is that abroad they don't hesitate to engage in simple jobs, some wash dishes in restaurants and bars, they clean city streets…but they refuse to do these jobs back home, they repel from doing them.

Socrates: Strange.

Andocides: Our villages are complaining of scarcity of land labors…agriculture is being neglected…and the agricultural lands have turned into arid lands…villages have come to rely on the city for food…I mean on what is imported…our agricultural country is no more agricultural, and destruction has spread.

Socrates: And you attribute all that owing to my meditation… and loathing of handiwork?

Andocides: I remind you of one other thing…remember the day you found a rat in your school…and one of your students tried to kill it…you scolded him, asked him to pity it…in many soft words?

Socrates: I may have done that one day.

Andocides: Since then, it has become a strict fashion…everybody was affected by you…have taken to raising rats and cuddling them in their homes.

Socrates: And what's wrong with that?

Andocides: Because of that, rats multiplied in thousands, or even millions in the agricultural fields…you find them on top of olive trees…gnawing its fruits…they dug themselves homes and tunnels in tree trunks…these rats have turned wild…have built whole colonies of rats…that no other creature can even come near it…even cats are no longer able to face them…People have become insensitive to eminent danger…they just let them devour all harvest. They may even spread plague around…

Socrates: Oh, wonder…the country is in hazard, and I'm not even aware of it!

Andocides: Because you're floating in your meditation…unaware of what's going on around you…and which is on account of your own doing.

Socrates: My own doing?

Andocides: For sure.

Socrates: Trust my word; had I known that my own life could save this nation, I wouldn't have hesitated to offer my life willingly.

Andocides: There, Socrates, you've reached the logical conclusion yourself.

Socrates: What do you mean?

Andocides: There is no hope for salvation from all these ills, except with your disappearance. (**To Democratia and the jury**) Members of the jury, for the sake of the common good and for the love of our homeland… not in spite of Socrates…I ask the honorable court…the verdict of sentence to death.

Democratia: Do you have anything else to say, Socrates?

Socrates: I have a strong desire to cry, but my tears won't obey.

Democratia: Alright, you have the time to weep…later…but now…it's time for election of the verdict. (**Addressing the jury**) Let each one of you write - without mentioning the name - the verdict you have reached, on the ostracon in his hand…innocence…or death.

(Addressing one of the ushers) As for you, you are to collect the ostraca in this pot. **(He takes the pot, approaches Democratia who writes her verdict on the ostracon)** As for me, write my name on this ostracon, as I am the head of this court. **(She throws the ostracon into the pot, the rest of the jury members follow; the usher closes the pot, places it before Democratia, who takes the lid off; checks the ostraca and announces the written verdict on each one of them, putting each category alone)** Innocent… innocent… innocent… death… innocent… death… innocent… innocent… death… death… death… **(Pauses)** death.

One of those sitting in the hall: Well…well…innocence equals that of death.

Another from the hall: Six votes here and six there.

A third from the hall: And what now?

A fourth from the hall: I think that equality is to be taken to the advantage of the defendant, I mean Socrates is innocent.

A fifth from the hall: Frankly it's puzzling…there are two sayings **(Noise)**

Democratia: **(Knocking her cane)** Athenians, you forget that the justice that was founded by the goddess Athena holds that in case votes are equal, the votes that include that of the head of the court outnumber, doesn't it?

Every one in the hall: Hail justice… hail justice.

Democratia: Then let us look for the ostracon of the head of the court… my humble person, **(Searches in the ostraca)** this is my verdict **(Raises the ostracon)** death. **(Complete silence, looks of horror and grief; here and there on the stage and in the hall; a spot of light focuses on Socrates)**

Socrates: As long as the honorable court…that represents the voice of the people…and the authority of the law…has said its word with my death…welcome to death that your virtuous city offers me. And if the salvation of this city lies in my death, welcome to this death…that will offer me eternity…and now the time has come for us to part…each in a separate road…you to carry on in the path of life…and me to the hereafter…which is the better, your destiny or mine? Only god knows.

(The Curtain)

Scene III

The Real Beginning

(The prison; a wide opening in the midst of the rock, graded from the top of the front part of the stage to its middle, on top of which the Acropolis columns can be seen in the far end; the houses of the city of Athens; in the middle of the prison is a stone seat that Socrates uses now and again; light suggests shortly after sunset).

Chief of guards: (**Addressing Socrates**) I have been working here in this prison for thirty years…and have never treated a prisoner as I've treated you…yes…we're soft with you Socrates to a great extent…keep no food or drink from you…visits for you are continuous, your students call on you day and night…as if living with you…no beating nor torturing… (**Going towards Socrates, holding him by the shoulder**) In Sparta they hold the prisoner by head, shake him like this (**Shakes Socrates twice then leaves him**), all day and night till he loses consciousness and probably his eye-sight, and he confesses what they want him to reveal.

Socrates: (**Moving away**) And does the prison law allow beating and torture? Or do you receive orders?

Chief of guards: We don't need a law or an order… whoever enters this prison becomes under our control… with no supervision on us…and we believe that prison is reform and rehabilitation.

Socrates: And this is what you seek by beating and torturing and loss of consciousness and sight?

Chief of guards: No…actually we seek no definite aim… what's important, is that the prisoner be obedient.

Socrates: Obedient! To the state laws?

Chief of guards: No…to us… we here are the state.

Socrates: So you're a state within the state?

Chief of guards: Say what you will…the important thing is that they all fear us…including the leaders themselves, for there may come a day when they find themselves here like the worst of criminals and yourself.

Socrates: This may be true… but I'm not afraid of you, even though I'm at your mercy… (**Adding**) although I respect you as executors of the law.

Chief of guards: It is our mistake.

Socrates: How is that?

Chief of guards: You haven't seen our power…you don't know the rules of prison…haven't tasted what other prisoners have…we spoilt you too much…actually, you are no prisoner.

Socrates: Why?

Chief of guards: I must admit that on learning of your coming, I rejoiced and prepared you a special program…full of all the arts of discipline…and various sorts of torture…

Socrates: And why all this interest and generosity?

Chief of guards: To me…you represent a unique prisoner…a truly typical case…a man of seventy…sentenced to death…after being convicted by all the people in the city…represented in the Areopagus Court staff, I mean you have wronged the whole state.

Socrates: (**As though to himself**) I like it how you place public duty as a law before your personal desires…indeed you're a good citizen…how wonderful to have a real guard in the ideal city!

Chief of guards: Before any thing else…I want vendetta.

Socrates: Vendetta…with me?

Chief of guards: My son…my only son…you've corrupted him…you ruined my home…he took you as his tutor…only to turn out as an intellectual…my son…my only son an intellectual…isn't this catastrophic? He neither learnt a useful craft…nor did he inherit my career as a prison warden…his mother is weeping day and night…for he is, like yourself, a vagrant…wandering through the alleys…meditating on everything that interests him or doesn't…my son…an intellectual! I swear by the gods that his destiny will ultimately turn out like you…here in prison… (**Three security guards enter; they salute**).

Security guard 1: We receive new orders.

Security guard 2: Weird…strange orders.

Security guard 3: These, sir, are the orders (**Hands him a piece of parchment**).

Chief of guards: (**Reads it**) "In the name of the people and of democracy we, governor of Athens and head of its supreme court, we order for the withdrawal of guards completely from Socrates' prison. This decree is to be carried out immediately on its report." (**He wraps the letter**) Oh, god! This is a catastrophic matter! What happened! An appraisal! (**After a moment of thought**) Guards! Attention! (**The guards stand in a row attentive**) In the name of the people, forward march! (**They start to march retreating from Socrates' prison**)

Socrates: (**Stopping them**) Guards of the ideal city…courageous Chief of guards, stand a moment! How can you leave me on my own! I have become used to you… Chief of guards…I have great respect for you, for to me you represent the law… (**They walk away**) Chief of guards…in the name of the gods…I implore you…to explain to me…the matter.

Chief of guards: If Socrates doesn't understand, do you think I will?

Socrates: (**Clings to the Chief of guards as the rest halt**) So, it's chaos… they leave the prisoners unguarded.

Chief of guards: But it's your prison only… this never happened before… this is a unique precedent.

Socrates: And why do they always treat me in this unique manner? Is it a sort of torture…they know how I respect and obey the law…so they break it before my eyes?

Chief of guards: I don't think so.

Socrates: Then what is the reason…? (**All the guards whisper for a while**)

Chief of guards: Anyway, you've got the right to know now…today is the nineteenth of the month, I think.

Socrates: Today is the eighteenth, is it time to go? …then I am ready.

Chief of guards: It is we who will depart from your prison… as for you, you will not.

Socrates: What are you hiding? In the name of the gods of Olympus… I implore you…tell me.

Chief of guards: A huge demonstration took place in the public meeting place… and in the streets of Athens.

Socrates: A demonstration… this is a new term I have never heard before.

Chief of guards: I mean citizens grouped and walked in rows… calling for your release.

Socrates: This is rude!

Chief of guards: And they went to Areopagus Court where you were trialed, and burnt it.

Socrates: That is backwardness and barbarian!

Chief of guards: Then they went into your school where they sat…and then the authorities surrounded the school and blew it up.

Socrates: Good for the authorities, law and order is above all.

Chief of guards: But citizens all around the city burst in chaotic anger, took to the streets as though they totally lost their senses, destroying everything around them…including barrels of liquor…stores of crops…everything…disorder spread everywhere and fire broke out…cries rose high, that the death sentence on Socrates was basically wrong.

Socrates: So Athens is lost…fallen into a waste abyss.

Chief of guards: The strange thing is that Chaerephon, your old friend, bearer of the oracle, was found killed in his home…rumors spread that he committed suicide… anyway whether he was killed or had committed suicide… doesn't matter.

Socrates: The Athenian people…gentle and kind...are they doing all that? This has never happened in the history of this ancient country. I wonder how any citizen can dare stand against his country's laws.

Chief of guards: Even if they are unfair?

Socrates: Fair or unfair, that's something no one person can decide…what's important is that what the nation decides becomes an obligatory law for everybody. (**Adding**) And of course, I don't accept using force with demonstrations… this, in itself, is against the law.

Chief of guards: How?

Socrates: The law commits both the ruler and the ruled to abide by it, it were better for the state to apply the law…instead of using force against the demonstration …otherwise, in itself it will be breaking the law.

Chief of guards: Well done …well done Socrates **(Whispering)** because my son was with them…**(Adding)** anyway…I don't want you to drag me into talking about politics, Socrates, besides, I've got to carry out orders… immediately… immediately. (**To the rest of the guards**) In the name of the people and the law attention…forward march(**They retreat leaving Socrates)**

Socrates: **(In a moment of meditation)** Ye gods… how did you create this Hellenic people!? I can't believe the myth that says that these people were made too late, or after the gods had made the universe and the humans. They sat to rest, took to toy and play, and in a whim they created the forefather of this species. But after they came back to their senses regretted what they had done, tried to destroy that species, so that they surrounded them with other people who loathed them, fought them - like the Persians - and when this didn't work out, they created another Hellenic species which they put inside the first, to fight it, and bite through its bones and so you find all Hellenic people everywhere speaking of Hellenic nationalism, making zealous speeches about unity, as the aspired aim and the promised dream, claiming the unity of the nation, as they share one religion and one language, same special characteristics, whereas the reality of the situation tells differently. For they are warring and disputing amongst themselves with no hope for unification. Athens is the biggest of these Hellenic cities bearing the vices of all of them, always paying a high price, or it wouldn't have reached its present degradation to the extent that the Athenian individuals are outlaws openly without remorse or even fear. My heart bleeds of pity over this devastated city where the fire of mutiny has ignited. **(After a moment's pause)** I am positively sure I'm innocent, for the trial was just a form and the accusations a frame up. I can almost smell foul play. But still, I am an example to the Athenians in abiding by the law, for whoever feels that he is a victim of oppression, the law is to be obeyed whatever the price. **(After a pause)** Pity the sun has set, and I am left in the dark.

(Leans his head on the Acropolis rock, dozes off a little, darkness is followed by soft light; a phantom approaches Socrates).

Socrates: **(To himself)** Who's there coming from far! .Is it a phantom? Or is he the god who guards me, who has come disguised? Yes, I wish he were to advise me of a law to save this nation from the distress that has befallen it! Or perhaps, it is death that comes to free me from my cares. Enough shame for me, that Athenians are being killed because of me! (**The phantom approaching slowly, Socrates addresses him**) You look strange, your figure is suspicious, why are you so silent like that! Speak out! Say something! (**The phantom almost touches Socrates who thinks he is a man**) Speak man! Who are you!?

__________: (**In a rough voice**) Citizen of Athens.

Socrates: Welcome to the prison of Socrates…though your voice is not natural, you seem to be one of the trouble-makers who spread chaos in the city…you were screaming with them all day till your voice became hoarse…didn't it?

__________: Do you call them trouble- makers?

Socrates: Anyone who raises his voice in the face of the law, and uses violence against the state is a sinful trouble-maker.

__________: But they support you, they love you, they want to set you free.

Socrates: And this adds to my misery. I feel I'm the cause of this violence and segregation (**The phantom uncovers his face to reveal Democratia**)

Democratia: Socrates…Socrates…you… (**Falls at his feet**)

Socrates: Democratia herself in my prison! (**He raises her up**) This is an unexpected honor…

Democratia: Socrates… you are a god, Socrates.

Socrates: (**Smiling**) A god! Don't forget you were at the head of the court that convicted me of atheism and what you say now could put you in the same convictions' cage, and with the same accusation! (**Laughs**)

Democratia: Socrates… the people's love for you has raised you to the status of deities…

Socrates: But people love you more than they love me…

Democratia: Socrates, enough ridiculing me… you know that the elections in our country are only a game; I mean it's not right. But when people go out to the streets in their naked chests… putting their lives at stake, crying your name against the will of the government, these are the real popular elections, and the truth that crystallizes the gods' love and care for you… love of the people means love of deities. Socrates you are an immortal god.

Socrates: But shortly I shall die, and people will forget it all.

Democratia: That is why I came.

Socrates: I don't understand…why?

Democratia: It is I who ordered the guards to be withdrawn from your prison.

Socrates: This is a mistake punished by the law.

Democratia: But the whole city is calling for your acquittal…and the peoples' request becomes the law we must obey.

Socrates: And there's a legal verdict against me.

Democratia: That is the fix we've fallen into…for I can neither abolish the sentence of the court I headed …nor am I able to carry out this verdict, for it will break out violence in the city.

Socrates: I see otherwise.

Democratia: How?

Socrates: Submission to the demands of the trouble-makers means submitting to violence…and this may become a rule that ruins our democracy, for everyone who has a certain interest and everyone who wishes to impose his will this attitude must be stopped immediately.

Democratia: You're right…in the case these demands are individual or sectarian or even small vocational…but the demands of the Athenian people are quite just.

Socrates: You mean to set me free?

Democratia: Yes…and now we are all convinced of the justness of your case.

Socrates: This means…that you and your government did not believe in my case until after the voice of the people rose…and this means that even this conviction in our country can only take place through violence and force…by demonstrations and acts of riot.

Democratia: There is a suitable solution.

Socrates: And what is that?

Democratia: The government will shut its eyes, allowing the peoples' demands a chance.

Socrates: That is a puzzle.

Democratia: Haven't you understood yet what I mean?

Socrates: Forgive me, I am slow in these matters.

Democratia: I'll say it quite clearly, and in all frankness…we have withdrawn the guards from your prison, to enable you to go out of here, in order to live.

Socrates: But I'll be going out of here to death, not to life, and this for me is better.

Democratia: Please try to understand me.

Socrates: You mean for me to escape secretly from here…under the very nose of the government?

Democratia: And we, the government, will pretend not to see or hear…escape, my brother.

Socrates: And where to?

Democratia: The world is so wide… (**A moment of pause**) We'll prepare for you the most modern and luxurious of our ships…and you'll travel secretly to anywhere you like…any country in the world.

Socrates: You offer me exile and misery then, on a golden plate.

Democratia: No for the love of gods! I came to save you from death. And we'll offer you a comfortable life anywhere you choose.

Socrates: But death within the walls of Athens and burial in its earth is a hundred times better than living thousands of years in the world's vast paradises that you speak of… Democratia, may you know that there is no life or death for Socrates outside Athens…my homeland is my birth and my death however may I be: whether an oppressor or a victim of oppression, happy or unhappy.

Democratia: As long as you love Athens that much…then defend it from splitting. (**Adding**) Anyway you can leave for some time, till things cool down, then come back.

Socrates: I can neither fool people nor life… nor do I risk my love for Athens.

Democratia: **(In despair)** Is this possible, that the gates of prison to be open up for you and you shut them yourself?

Socrates: Yes, because a closed prison is more welcome to me than a life I am offered with treachery or deceit, or by violating the law…I am a free-willed prisoner…so if you set me free you will have robbed me of my will, my being, my very existence.

Democratia: Then we'll put back the guards once more.

Socrates: This is better for me and you…at least you'll be abiding by the physical shape of matters…

Democratia: **(As if to herself)** Then the problem will remain unsolved… **(Raises her voice)** Socrates…what are your final conditions…to go out of prison?

Socrates: I have no conditions…for I will never go out of prison alive…leave me …don't spoil my solitude… in these last minutes of my life.

Democratia: Are these your last words?

Socrates: Yes…I came here on a legal order, and I'll not leave this place without it.

Democratia: **(Comes closer to Socrates, her voice trembling)** Socrates…it seems you despise me?

Socrates: You must know, my lady, that he who has respect for himself, doesn't despise others…and who am I to despise the chief of the state?

Democratia: **(Her voice trembling more)** So why do you turn your face away? Why don't you look me in the eye? Socrates… you are a god, Socrates.

Socrates: I am surprised at the ease with which you deify humans! Anyway, you remind me of the oracle that claimed me as the wisest of the wise…so don't repeat that to me again. I'm sick of it.

Democratia: But I want to confess to you…

Socrates: What of?

Democratia: It is I who forged the oracle… I wanted to exploit your abilities and authority on the peoples' minds… I sent Chaerephon and planned it, so that he returns from Delphi with a false oracle.

Socrates: So at last the truth is unveiled…thank you, my friend…it was a perplexing question that concerned me all my life…and now you have answered it in a definite and satisfying way.

Democratia: Then you are glad to discover the falsehood of the oracle?

Socrates: Indeed…and what comforts me is that I am the only one not to be fooled by this oracle…all the people believed it and I refuted it… it was this oracle that led me to prison.

Democratia: And it has also uplifted you to the status of a deity.

Socrates: You're back to saying nonsense.

Democratia: **(Ignoring his answer)** Because you, you knew that corruption was spreading throughout the country, without leaving the smallest glimpse of hope for reform, you insist on giving an example. I'm almost sure that you believe in your innocence and still insist on carrying out the law

Socrates: Do you know the secret of our crisis, Democratia? Each person has no trust in the other…each one sees the other as corrupt…so he doesn't expect that things will go on in accordance with its normal course. Everything has to be maneuvered. It's all right to pay bribes…in governmental circles …and in order to be able to pay bribes, you got to have other resources…so it's all right to swindle and fraud…and so goes on and on in an endless circle…

Democratia: That's right…so what's the solution?

Socrates: I'll tell you a tale that I heard from my grandmother… who said she had heard from her grandmother. The tale says that in a very ancient state…which is the most ancient in the world… maybe Egypt… corruption abided and souls degenerated as is the case we are having now, or even worse.

Democratia: **(Interrupting)** I don't think there's worse than our state.

Socrates: **(Adding)** The ruler went and walked among the people, dialogued with them, the bribed one told him: "Why should I refuse a bribe? I take it because if I don't …it'll go to someone else". The embezzler told him: "Do you expect me to leave the money that someone else may steal?". The oppressor told him: "He who doesn't oppress people will himself be oppressed". The private tutor who charges huge fees for his private lessons and doesn't work hard in his school said: "Why should I work hard…to stop private lessons…

while someone else is compiling money, built high buildings out of private lessons? I myself pay a lot of money to my children's tutors." And so answered the rest of the people.

Democratia: And that's exactly what is happening here.

Socrates: The ruler returned to the castle…thought deeply into the matter…and announced to the people the outcome he had reached. He offered them three months to reconsider… then decided on a certain hour on a certain day…to the point that every person stopped being afraid of the other…that each man would stop committing mistakes unto others…for one single whole day…the national discipline day…he called it conscience day. Everybody responded, trying that "conscience day"…when no bribes were taken…no embezzling or any illegal trespasses…and each one of them felt safe with the other…things at governmental circles and elsewhere went on fine.

Democratia: And what happened then?

Socrates: The ruler spoke to them, asked them if they wished that everyday of the year would be as "conscience day". They unanimously agreed. It is said that this ancient state whether it was Egypt, or elsewhere, was redressed and its civilization prospered.

Democratia: And do you think that we can do this in Athens?

Socrates: On my part, I started with myself…my very insistence on carrying out the verdict, and on staying in prison till death, is but for that goal…our society, Democratia, is in dire need of a model…

Democratia: (Approaching Socrates) That's right, Socrates.

Socrates: **(Yawning)** True… I can't resist **(Leans his head on the Acropolis rock, sitting crouching and dozes off)**.

Democratia: **(Staring in Socrates' face)** This is the peace of the deities… the comfort of the virtuous. You were fair Socrates and therefore you sleep in calmness **(Kisses Socrates' forehead, enter both Xanthula and Hedone, Xanthula is carrying her infant; Hedone is holding the two other boys' hands; stands at a distance)**.

Hedone: Shame… catastrophe…a beautiful woman is kissing the sleeping Socrates!

Xanthula: I don't believe it.

Hedone: You don't believe it…but you see it!?

Xanthula: Perhaps…

Hedone: Perhaps…perhaps…! There is a woman sleeping in the arms of the man…kissing him, sister…and you say perhaps! …ah…my misery…if I were in your shoes, I'd kill him here and now.

Xanthula: Mind your words, Hedone… for we're visiting my husband who is sentenced to death.

Hedone: **(A little calmer)** Sorry, my lady…but the problem is that we have done everything possible… we went out at night…crossed the dark roads to visit him…only to find him sleeping in the arms of another woman, which means he hasn't slept all night…let's go back…come again in the daytime **(Starts to leave)**.

Xanthula: **(Holding her)** There must be some mistake… **(Socrates' snoring rises)** Can't you see that my husband is fast asleep?

Hedone: In case of suspicion, this very snoring can be even more dubious…for men don't fall into deep slumber like that, unless they're worn out…as for satisfaction, well it is up to you, to say the first and last word in this matter.

Xanthula: Are you crazy?

Hedone: A man and a woman sleeping in the arms of Acropolis…night befalls on them…and you call me crazy.

Xanthula: Alright, let's go closer to them, for I can't believe that Socrates would join with a woman unless she's a descendant of the gods.

Hedone: Oh grief… the goddess of beauty descends from Olympus to sleep in the arms of Socrates in the midnight! And you call me crazy!

Xanthula: Stupid…gods do what they please…and we are to accept their judgment.

Hedone: So what will you do, my virtuous woman?

Xanthula: **(Approaching the sleeping woman who was leaning her head on Socrates' lap; Xanthula moves her head and steps back surprised)** Horror! This is strange! Democratia!

Hedone: Democratia! This woman is no virtuous, nor pure goddess…huh!

Xanthula: No… but maybe th…

Hedone: **(Interrupting)** Maybe…maybe…

Xanthula: I mean maybe they were discussing the matter of democracy… or of the disaster in the country… or the case of Socrates himself.

Hedone: Do you call this snoring a dialogue in democracy… and these embraces and kisses do you call them democratic discussions?

Xanthula: Hedone…let me give you a piece of information… all my life I have never once suspected Socrates… whatever differences between us were because of his engagement with his philosophy and students. That's all there is to it… he is a faithful man… reliable… only the spiteful would suspect Socrates.

Hedone: You're his wife…it's up to you.

Xanthula: It's better to move away a bit from them so as not to disturb their sleep…or stop their dialogue…if they dialogue with each other (**They are about to leave, but Democratia wakes up; points at her to stop, goes towards them**).

Democratia: Who? Xanthula?

Xanthula: Say nothing… I would never suspect Socrates… Aphrodite, the goddess of beauty herself, cannot tempt him.

Democratia: I don't know what you mean, but the situation is serious.

Xanthula: What I say is clear, but you are not.

Democratia: Please try to understand…at dawn…the sacred ship will reach the eastern port, and for which the death sentence on your husband has been postponed …now do you understand?

Xanthula: Yes…so what can we do?

Democratia: He must be set saved.

Hedone: (**Sarcastic and whispering**) And is this what you came to do, leader? To set Socrates free requires sleeping in his arms?

Xanthula: (**In a loud voice**) Shut up, Hedone! Have you gone out of your mind?

Democratia: (**Takes Xanthula stands aside**) I've withdrawn the guards from the prison of Socrates.

Hedone: (**Interrupting**) Well done, or we would have paid a huge bribe to be here…besides the advantage of seeing in private a man about to die.

Xanthula: **(Doggedly)** Scram from my face, Hedone! I told you to shut up.

Democratia: **(Carrying on)** You've got to convince him to leave before the break of dawn…there's a ship in the western port waiting for him…let him take it away from our shores…to carry him to any island.

Xanthula: But I can't bear leaving him to go away from me.

Hedone: **(To herself)** My wonder!

Democratia: You can join him later on…what's important now is that he leaves.

Xanthula: Then I'll go wake him up.

Democratia: If he departs before sunrise, then he and the whole state will be saved, god bless you Xanthula, do what we agreed upon…now. **(She exits, Xanthula approaches Hedone)**

Hedone: I don't understand what's going on here... everybody is acting in a strange manner…we're not used to that.

Xanthula: Sit here…with the boys…and I'll go with the infant to Socrates.

Hedone: Will you sleep in his lap?

Xanthula: Shut up! Enough joking! **(Smiling)** I'll wake him up my way. I know my husband well. **(Approaches Socrates, sits beside him, touches his forehead; closes up more and more; kisses him but discovers a louse on his bald, picks it up, kills it with her nails in the manner of a peasant)** I told you dear… to take care of yourself…you never heard me…lice were walking on your body…**(Looks on his head once more; he wakes up slowly; as soon as he spots his wife, he stands up terrorized)**

Socrates: Oh, my horror! That terrible nightmare never leaves me!

Xanthula: It's neither a nightmare nor a dream… it's real my dear.

Socrates: Who…you! Then everything is in danger! You have come to spoil my prison…to narrow its space on me, make me lose the pleasure of meditation in my last moments.

Xanthula: Meditate… meditate, my dear this is what has brought you to the point of having lice.

Socrates: Can't you postpone your talking for two or three days…!?

Xanthula: Impossible…you have got to listen to me before your departure…besides I'll be accompanying you.

Socrates: Accompany me! This means you'll never let me go till after death.

Xanthula: Of course.

Socrates: So you wish to die with me?

Xanthula: Me and the children too.

Socrates: **(Mocking)** And why go into all this trouble?

Xanthula: No, dear. **(Pulls him)** Know that I'm your wife… **(Approaches him)** I've changed completely, Socrates, I've come to appreciate you and to wish you a long life.

Socrates: Impossible!

Xanthula: (Stares into his eyes) I beg you to forgive all I've done throughout our marital life.

Socrates: On my part…I forgave you quite a long time ago… I keep for you only the best of feelings…for you're the mother of my children… only I had wished you to accompany me on the path of virtue

Xanthula: That's what I'm trying to do now.

Socrates: It's too late…for in a few minutes I'll die and that's the end of everything.

Xanthula: No…you won't die.

Socrates: Will you oppose me even in death…

Xanthula: I beg you!

Socrates: The matter is out of hand.

Xanthula: Not only do me and my children need you…but all the sons of Athens…you don't know, Socrates how you've affected me and all hearts…your students' demonstrations… everybody without exception, are shouting for you…the very roads and alleys of Athens…everything in the city would bend on its knees to beg you to stay alive…**(Bows to kiss his feet)** Socrates you are my husband…and my master…and father of my children …Socrates you are my god…Socrates(**She cries**).

Socrates: This is no time to cry, my dear wife... **(Pats her on the shoulder)**.

Xanthula: Then listen to my begging: I have but one request for you... not to surrender to death...or else, take me with you...

Socrates: Ask for what you want...I'll fulfill all your desires... except this request...it's impossible.

Xanthula: It is a popular request.

Socrates: Law is above any requests, the people themselves must submit to the law.

Xanthula: Look at this infant, how can he live as an orphan?

Socrates: I have left him what will safeguard him, his freedom...he and his peers (**Plato enters**).

Plato: Good morning, my professor.

Socrates: Good morning, Plato...what brings you here...I understand you're ill?

Plato: In a few hours the sun will rise...then I shall be riding the seas heading for Egypt...at the same time you will be on your immortal trip.

Xanthula: **(Interrupts crying)** Plato, my son...do you agree that easily that your tutor surrenders to death?

Plato: Had I done otherwise...I wouldn't be a true student to this great professor.

Xanthula: You can save him...take him with you to Egypt.

Plato: I wouldn't think of that...nor would he do it...law to Socrates is the great god of every social system...to him if there is no law, there is no life...and Socrates who dies now, gives meaning to life where there was not. He is igniting the fire of the Athenian torch, that has turned off into ashes, let him die, my lady.

Xanthula: This is nonsense...for to resist injustice, doesn't come by surrendering to a law imposed by oppressors.

Socrates: But the verdict made against me represented the majority.

Plato: A misleading majority... You mean a misleading majority.

Socrates: So let it be…as long as the verdict has been made against me, I must carry it out, that the people may get used after I am gone, to respecting the law. When will the day come when our people will honestly seek to carry out the law if even on themselves?

Plato: This is actually a dream to all of us.

Socrates: Anyway, you will depart with sunrise?

Plato: Yes… I've come to bid you the final farewell. (**Hugs him**) And know, my professor that I am going to Egypt to acquire of its knowledge and wisdom, to start writing about you… and explain your ideas, which you have implanted within our souls, without writing it in a book. I will be your immortal book.

Socrates: I wish you wouldn't do what Herodotus did…he limited his visits to the temples…mixed only with priests…relied on translators. Better my son to learn their language and mix with the common people, rather than the élite, better still if you'd learn their language…try to wander throughout the Egyptian countryside…there you can learn Egyptian wisdom in its purest and most wonderful form…for the simple Egyptian peasant has learned from nature itself…and thus acquiring from it transparency. He grew up in the arms of the Nile…and hence his generosity, sweated as he planted the land, threw the seeds…dug the small canals, flattened the roads…built pyramids…that is the Egyptian peasant of the most profound wisdom known by the ancient peoples. He is a smart, kind, clever, wise and mature, elegant, slim…handsome and clean…Plato can you do that?

Plato: I'll do my best…though I'm worried about the difficulty of the Egyptians' language and the depth of their wisdom. But I've relations in Naucratis, west of the Delta…I will be their guest…whereby I'll learn the language, if I can.

Socrates: May the gods grant you luck.

Plato: And now I bid you farewell with the gods of Olympus and the Underworld together… my professor, I 'm leaving for Egypt and you're on your way to immorality…farewell wisest of the wise. **(Cries)**

Socrates: Farewell…this is an hour of joy, not of weeping…look, Plato at the sun rising and smile (**Adding**) Plato, take Xanthula with her children to our home…it's on your way to the port…don't leave her here for she doesn't stop crying. (**Looks at Xanthula**) Farewell, my dear wife... take good care of our children... (**Xanthula breaks down staring at Socrates in astonishment; Plato pulls her, she leaves without uttering a word; whereas Hedone's tears pour; the Chief of guards enters dressed in red**).

Chief of guards: Good morning, Socrates.

Socrates: Good morning, Chief of guards.

Chief of guards: No rather Head of state.

Socrates: And how is that?

Chief of guards: I've learnt my lesson from you, Socrates.

Socrates: I don't understand.

Chief of guards: I've learnt from you that the sovereignty of the law is the foundation of any progress, so I made a revolution and threw off Democratia, imposed law and order on the city.

Socrates: O pity! All human crimes are committed in the name of the law...what amazes me, is the fact that you're pinning your ill deeds on me...for I call for respect of the law, while you are acting outside the limits of the law, and claim that my teachings inspired you.

Chief of guards: Socrates...try to understand...I made a revolution with the aim of restoring the law its respect... and to confirm the foundations of democracy...and I'll abide by the consultation.

Socrates: But surely you have gagged mouths?

Chief of guards: Temporary procedures...besides, all I did was to order my guards to arrest every one who considers objecting to the state's laws, if even by one word.

Socrates: This is aggression and despotism.

Chief of guards: Temporary despotism is far better than false democracy.

Socrates: You mean forging the latest democratic elections?

Chief of guards: Yes...for the former leaders came into office by forgery ...I came into the office by the swords' edge. Which one is better?

Socrates: Rather say which is worse...there's neither good in either.

Chief of guards: Have you a better idea?

Socrates: What do you mean?

Chief of guards: I am power…and you are wisdom…come join me in governing and in undertaking responsibility, for no one can oppose me now. I can set you free and abolish the death verdict against you…and I'll leave you to walk through the streets…make a dialogue with your students…only convince them with my good will, and tell them that I'm trying to rebuild true democracy in the country.

Socrates: But whoever comes into authority the manner you did, is not to be trusted…nor will any good come out of him, his promises are not true, nor will he keep his words…you're a dictator.

Chief of guards: Only a few moments left before your execution…think fully, but consider things well.

Socrates: Leave me alone…and let the pure eye of the sun see me with its brightness…I am not ashamed to meet the sun face to face…for its purity reflects in my eyes…my face blooms from her freshness. As for you and your deeds, you soil the sun's rays, pollute the atmosphere and the environment around us…go away. I thank gods I'll be going where there is no room for the likes of you.

Chief of guards: Then you insist on your opinion… (**Addresses the guards**) Bring forth the cup of poison…let him drink it completely that he may rest and give relief. (**A guard leaves and returns quickly with the cup, moves towards Socrates, and before he hands it to him, takes a sip, falls dead quickly; Socrates rushes and holds the cup in his hand, as everyone stands motionless in his place, speechless**).

Socrates: (**Wanders with his eyes around the places; stares at the Acropolis and the Athenian houses; then at the sun, takes the cup close to his mouth**) In the name of the homeland… in the name of true democracy… in the name of the law, I drink this cup to the last sip, I am not less grieved than anyone who leaves life, but the call of duty is stronger to me than any other call…so farewell… farewell… (**Drops all the cup at once in his mouth, falls dead immediately, his head falling on the Acropolis, while the cup is still firm on his mouth**).

(The Curtain)